Funny Conversations with God

Funny Conversations with God

An Uncalled-For Dialogue

Dunn Neugebauer

iUniverse, Inc.
Bloomington

Funny Conversations with God
An Uncalled-For Dialogue

iUniverse books may be ordered through booksellers or by contacting:

iUniverse
1663 Liberty Drive
Bloomington, IN 47403
www.iuniverse.com
1-800-Authors (1-800-288-4677)

ISBN: 978-1-4759-5086-1 (sc)
ISBN: 978-1-4759-5085-4 (hc)
ISBN: 978-1-4759-5084-7 (e)

Library of Congress Control Number: 2012917625

Printed in the United States of America

iUniverse rev. date: 09/28/2012

Contents

Acknowledgments

Hey, God, do you think this book will ever get published?

This isn't the time for that! This is the part where you thank all of the people who made this manuscript possible. Come on, granite head! Quit being so selfish!

So this section is sort of like the Academy Award speeches?

Gosh no! The Academy Awards are _way_ too long! Please keep it short and to the point. Besides, people are busy! They don't have time to read a five-page acknowledgment! Start thanking people … and fast. I've got a lot going on right now in this world!

Hold on. I'm climbing onto the stage right now, adjusting the microphone.

Get over yourself! You're sitting at home in your Donald Duck pajamas!

Great! Thanks for sharing that with everyone.

You hope there's an "everyone!" Please hurry; some Olympic swimmers are calling my name right now, and a second baseman just

singled in Miami. For some reason he wants special attention. Man, these athletes sometimes!

Good evening, everyone!

If you don't quit, I'm going to leave you!

You said you'd never leave me.

Actually I'm not, though you are seriously trying my patience! You do that sometimes, you know.

Well … to start with, wouldn't I thank myself? After all, I'm the one who wrote it!

Ahem!

And of course I'd like to thank you. Without you … well … I don't want to think about that.

No, you don't! Wherever would you be if I didn't send you your frozen TV dinners and your coffee with way too much sugar you drink every morning? And don't get me started on the simple things, like keeping our planets in order and keeping the sun from getting carried away and frying you all!

Sure, thanks for that.

You're welcome! And you'd like to thank …

I'd like to thank both my brothers, for starters—Mark for his support and Chip for convincing me to keep going with this. I almost scrapped this project halfway through, you know.

Might've been a good thing!

I just love getting abused by God!

Just busting your chops. Anyway, the completed project happened because, after a two- or three-month layoff, you remembered to bring me back into your life. I could've made your whole life easier if you hadn't forgotten in the first place!

Really?

Yes, really. Now who else would you like to thank?

My friend and former doubles partner, Skip Johnson. He's been supportive, plus he's writing a book on gratitude as we speak that I hope sees the light of day. Gratitude rocks!

Good, keep going.

I'd like to thank my colleague and friend Peggy Shaw. She's been supportive in the entire process. Couldn't have done it without her. Also, props go out to my good friend and "adopted father" Pride Evans and my running friend, Jan Gross. She brought up this book after I'd given up on it. She motivated me to continue. Jill Ellington is another – she helped a lot with the editing.

And?

And can I be serious for a second?

No, not really. That doesn't work well for you.

Thanks. Anyway, I'd like to end by being grateful that I finished the project. Usually I'm one who starts something but doesn't finish.

Like your marriage, for instance?

I was hoping you weren't going to bring that up.

If my memory is correct, you're going to talk about that in this manuscript.

Yes, I am. That's another thing to thank you for—getting me over that.

You're welcome once again. Anyway, is that all?

No! I'd like to thank all the potential publishers and agents who rejected me. That made me work even harder!

Wow ... good ... original even!

Thanks! Now, I hate to do this to you, but I'm going to be the one to cut this thing short.

You, why? What do you have to do that's so important?

The Braves game just started.

Good grief!

Often, that's exactly what it leads to.

Okay, let's get on with it then. No, wait ... hold on a second!

What?

Who's pitching?

Acknowledgments – Part II

On a serious note: Not only am I aware that a series of spiritual books entitled Conversations with God exists, but I am also here to tell you that those books changed my life. Though I have never been fortunate enough to meet the author, Neale Donald Walsch, if I did meet him, I would quickly shake his hand and thank him for his kind words and his courage to bring his manuscripts forward.

That being said, my manuscript is in *no way* intended to slander, belittle, or shoot down his fine works. Instead, my book is an attempt to carry his idea forward, though obviously in a different tone.

It happened this way for me: There's a conversation between Mr. Walsch and God in one of his books where Walsch tells God that he was thinking of writing a book called *What if God Were a Salami Sandwich.* God asks why he didn't write it, and Mr. Walsch's answer is that he thought it would be horribly irreverent. God answers by saying, "It would have been WONDERFULLY irreverent!" It was from this part of the book that my own idea came, and I simply took up the irreverent/wonderfully irreverent job of writing *Funny Conversations with God.*

In summary, I am thankful for Mr. Walsch and his conversations with the Man above. My own work is an extension—albeit a different one—of what he has started.

Thanks again, Neale Donald Walsch, and please keep up the good work!

The Beginning: Eerie Messages

It's January as I write this. Five inches of snow have fallen on our Atlanta grounds, and our city of over five million, as is usually the case when winter weather sets in, is in a panic. Because the city has only eight snow trucks—or eleven, depending on which media outlet you believe—I am stuck in my condo, unable to make my sacred walk to Dunkin' Donuts. Starting my day without my vanilla coffee with cream and teeth-rotting amounts of sugar is simply not a pleasant beginning.

Being socially challenged these days, I am snowed in with no one. My best friend of twenty years recently took a job in Beirut, my ex-wife has been gone for five years, and my nonphysical girlfriend just moved down to South Georgia to begin nursing school. And me without my one-thousand-piece Norman Rockwell jigsaw puzzles. Or my Advil. Instead, it's just me and CNN or reruns of *Two and a Half Men*, depending on my mood, along with piles of nasty TV dinners that should kill me if the snow doesn't.

Day one was okay, with the excitement of the newly fallen snow, the postcard-pretty landscapes, the knowing I wouldn't have to work for the next few days, and the quickly opened beer bottles that were slowly disappearing from my refrigerator. Somewhere in the middle of day two, however, things got ... well ... boring.

And don't get me started on days three through five.

But I digress.

Somewhere during day two, I started to ponder the meaning of all this—not the snow, but all of this in general. Questions started lining up

1

inside my head, each one begging for attention, feeling more important than the ones before. I could actually see the inner hands being raised in the mental classroom, begging to be acknowledged: Is there really a God? Is his name God, or does it really matter? Why can't I slice a serve wide to the ad side? Why is it impossible to throw up only once? And, more importantly, why are there so many episodes of *How I Met Your Mother* on TV lately? I mean, what's up with that?

As I settled deeper into my couch—if that was possible—a voice shouted into my head. I'm not sure why this was so surprising, but I actually jumped, as if the very noise was somehow out of place. I put down my stale milk, jammed my hand into my pocket, and yanked out my cell phone, spilling my lucky rock onto the floor in the process.

"Hello?"

"Hi, Dunn, it's God. You had some questions for me. Just thought I'd give you a holler to make an appointment with you. I just wanted to see if I could clear some things up."

Priding myself on my sense of humor, I didn't miss a beat. "Hi, God, where are you calling from?"

"I'm not on your phone; I'm in your head. What, did you think I was just trying out my new iPhone?"

"God has an iPhone?"

"Of course not; I've got other ways to keep up with the times! I did have a BlackBerry, though, but I dropped it and it broke. Couldn't get it to work after that for the life of me. You'd think—you know, with me being God and all—that I could've fixed it, but not this one. Once it went—man, it went."

I scratched my head, wondering just what I had had to drink the night before that made me deserve this. After making a mental inventory—three glasses of wine and one beer—I was satisfied it wasn't the drink, as I'd handled three or four of almost anything in the past. Still, who was this person, and why was he bothering me?

"Oh, I don't mean to be bothering you," the voice continued. "In fact, I've got to be running along. Got a war to deal with and some major flooding going on. Still, meet me tomorrow morning at eight a.m., pen and paper in hand, and we'll solve life's problems, you and I."

"We're doing what?" I asked.

"Tomorrow! Eight a.m. sharp! Pencil and paper! Be there!" And with that I heard a click inside my head. Game, set, match.

The Next Morning

"Wake up!"

I jumped out of the bed, wondering where this loud, screeching order had come from. Clutching my ears, I grabbed my phone and realized it hadn't rung. I leaped up, threw open the closets, and quickly peered under the bed. After squinting behind the window shades and wedging apart coat hangers, I was convinced nothing was in the room with me.

"It's me, God! I'm in your head. You were supposed to meet me this morning at eight a.m. sharp, remember?"

"What time is it?"

"It's nine twenty. You're over an hour late. Do you show up this late when you go on job interviews?"

Scratching my eyes and adjusting my Donald Duck pajamas, I immediately said, "Of course I'm always late. If I could be on time, I would never be looking for jobs!"

I heard laughter in my head—I guess from God—and I prided myself on being able to make the Great One chuckle. Making a mental check mark on my scorecard, I settled onto my bed.

"Get up! Go get your pad and paper; we've got some talking to do!" The voice was quieter, more tolerable, yet it sounded a bit bothered by my tardiness.

As I walked into the den, I felt weird and out of place talking to perhaps no one, but I talked anyway. "I'm sorry, God. You see, I just got a new phone. It's got all these app thingies on there—I can check the weather, talk to a friend in China, and even learn recipes for some dish I'll never make. I just don't know how to set the alarm. Can you help me?

"You're asking God if he knows how to work an iPhone?"

"Sorry, I guess that was a dumb question."

"You humans are usually taught that there are no dumb questions. In this case, however, I think I'll make an exception."

I laughed myself, peering under my recent copies of *Sports Illustrated* and *People*, searching quickly for a pen and paper. I succeeded, poised my pen at the top of a blank page, and waited—and waited.

"God, please don't leave me like this. It's a day off for me, and I haven't yet had my coffee. Could we start now? Or would you rather wait a few minutes and let me walk down to my coffee hole?"

"Ahem!" I heard, and it sounded a bit angry.

"Oh, there you are," I said. "I thought you'd left me."

"No, even though you kept me waiting over an hour, I'm still here. Oh, wait; hold on! A fellow just scored a goal in a soccer match overseas. He's making a signal to me and wants me to acknowledge it. Man, these sports people keep me busy doing that. Don't they know I've got better things to worry about? Wars, floods, famines, and I'm supposed to acknowledge it when they single up the middle or score a goal? The guy shouldn't be taking the credit anyway; it was a great pass! All he had to do was tap it in near post. To quote from you, what's up with that?"

"You mean you're not proud of him?" I asked, one of my first of many questions to the Man.

"His coach isn't! In fact, he's yelling at him right now, telling him to quit showboating. The coach has a point, by the way. I mean, just do your job. Act like you do it all the time. Georgia's old football great Herschel Walker was a great example. Did you notice what he would do after he scored a touchdown? He would hand the ball to the ref and then run off the field. He always modestly said it was because he was too tired to do anything else, but his attitude is something that should be copied. Do your job, don't show up the competition, and then go back to your huddle or your baserunning or whatever your job is."

"So we should all be like Herschel Walker?"

"In some ways, yes, and in other ways, no, which is *exactly* like all the rest of you. Imitate the good, dismiss the bad, and use the great brains I've given you! And quit always—and that is one word and two: all-ways—being dependent on what somebody else is trying to get you to do. I've given you all great talents; now use them! And you don't have to point up to me after you do something great; I know what you're doing. Just keep doing it, and thank me silently every now and then. I don't need a signal! In fact, I don't even want one!

"Is God irritated here?"

"I invented irritation! Where do you think it came from? But we're getting off the point. Let's get to your questions, and let's solve the world's problems. I've noticed you've called on me from time to time—mostly when you're trying to score with a female, I'm sorry to say—but I do hear your voice.

"I actually got down on my knees one time back when I was living up north."

"Up north?"

"Is there a problem with up north?"

"I'm always fascinated by you humans. You live on a perfectly round planet, yet you continually insist on there being a north, south, east, and west. How exactly does that happen? And why? And yes, I remember when you hit your knees. You were living in Lancaster, Pennsylvania, if I'm not correct—and I usually am, by the way.

"Then why did you send me up there? I was cold, I was lonely, I was depressed, I was divorced. They didn't even have comfortable chairs in Barnes & Noble for crying out loud! I felt like I'd died and gone to … well, never mind."

"You weren't in hell. Lancaster is a very nice place. It just wasn't the place for you."

"Then why did you send me up there? I even got rid of my wonderful dog to move up there. My dog! I got over my ex-wife, but I never, ever got over giving up my dog! I kick myself for it every day!"

"Something you should stop doing, by the way. Jasper is up here with me now, and he's doing fine. He enjoyed his time with you, even though

when you walked him you could've let him stay out a little longer. And …
go ahead and say it; I know why you're laughing."

"Of course you do; why wouldn't you? I was just wondering if he'd
corrected his little flaw. I mean, when he had to pee, he used to lift up his
back legs and then he'd pee all over his front ones. I used to laugh *every*
time—for ten years! He'd have this embarrassed look on his cute little
face, but it never failed. Up would go the back legs and then *splash*—all
over his front side."

"Bless his heart. Jasper is laughing with you now. He wants you to
know he's got it all worked out and his flaw in itself was perfect. He wanted
to make you laugh. He's always known at some level how important
laughing is to you. Hence the peeing "problem." He's peeing perfectly
now, by the way; no need for another splash. After all, his work with you
has already been perfectly done."

"Has he learned how to bark? I mean, Basenjis can't bark, you know.
What's up with that, by the way? Why invent a dog that can't bark? That
seems kind of cruel, don't you think?"

"Did you say cruel? Is it cruel that some men can't walk? Or talk?
Or hear? You don't know what they're trying to do on your planet.
People with defects—as you call them—do as much or more to teach
people than so called "normal" ones. But let's get back to your question:
why did I send you to Lancaster without your dog or your wife or your
collection of eighties movies? Why did I let you cast out of South Florida
with nothing but a full tank of gas and your bad seventies haircut? Oh,
and your iPod—which I finally taught you how to work, by the way.
Congrats on that! Even Jasper figured it out before you did, but that's
okay. I applauded your persistence. *Columbo* had nothing on you in that
case."

"*Columbo* rocked!"

"Thanks!"

"You wrote *Columbo*?"

"In earthly terms, no, but where do you think the idea came from?
And didn't Peter Falk do a great job? And who do you think helped Peter
Falk? Where do you think the ideas of the trench coat, the cigar, the beat-

up jalopy, and the wife you never saw came from? And the fact that you never, ever learned his first name!"

"What was his first name?"

"That's just it, he didn't have one. Though there was a Trivial Pursuit game that incorrectly gave him the name 'Philip.' I can assure you, though, that wasn't my doing. In fact, I wasn't very happy about that."

"Did you punish them?"

"What is it with you humans and punishment? Though there are earthly punishments for certain things, I feel you people do a more than adequate job—*much* more, by the way—of punishing yourselves. But let's get back to you and Pennsylvania."

"Let's. That was the longest eighty-nine days of my life, and yes, I did count."

"I know you did. After all, I made you a southern boy! Still, you needed those eighty-nine days—as you correctly counted—as they groomed you for the four years since you've moved back home."

"Why?"

"Because I needed to teach you gratitude. Do you realize how much better your lives would be if you dwelled on this emotion? Do you realize what a thriving planet yours would be? And no, I'm not talking about in college after you scored with Lisa Berkeley—that was her low esteem and morally-challenged times she was going through. You just happened to be at the "right" time and place. I'm talking about simple gratitude. If you want to send me a signal, don't wait till you've scored a goal or hit a homer; how about being a bit thankful for everything you've got. I mean, good me, make a list if you have to. Keep it in your pocket with that lucky rock of yours."

"Is that the only reason you sent me up there?"

"No, there are many. And I'm sure if you thought about it for a few seconds you could answer your own questions. Hey, could we pause again for a second?

"Another goal?"

"No, must be halftime. I'm going to try to talk a man off a ledge in Seattle, among other things. We need a small break anyway. Start a new chapter! I hate reading books where there either are no chapters or the chapters are really long. You people have short attention spans—not my fault—so end this chapter and start a new one. We can still pick up where we left off. Or not; I don't care. And by the way, start skipping a space where your question ends and my answer begins. It avoids confusion.

And So It Begins

~~~~~~~~~~~~~~~

Hey, God, let's set some ground rules while we're skipping spaces and all that. From now on, you get bold print because you're ... you know ... God. I'm demoted to regular print since you know about my sins, lies, lustful thoughts (is that a sin?), and other things. My editor, however, pointed out that until proof is provided, you could get demoted to standard type size as well, but somehow, I just didn't feel comfortable demoting God. My editor invited you to return to bold print only when you (1) send your son back or (2) part the Red Sea on CNN during prime time. You could also burn a bush. (Speaking of which, I've got a couple of Bushes I could recommend.)

Until then, we'll skip spaces, you get bold, I get "normal" print, and we'll go from there. Sound good?

I must say I couldn't care less.

Thanks, I think. But let's continue, though I feel guilty talking about me when there's so much wrong with the world.

Well, you are pretty whacked, but I do find you amusing in a demented sort of way. But go ahead; let's talk some more. I can split my attention when I need to, and you're usually good for a chuckle, whether you're trying to be funny or not.

Okay, here goes. First off, who's in charge when you go on vacation? I've heard it is Bear Bryant, but I don't want to start rumors.

Hey, you're pretty funny. I didn't know you were an Alabama fan. In fact, I'm God; I *know* you're not an Alabama fan. Why didn't you go back to Herschel Walker or your Columbo character? Or why not Tim Tebow? He played ball in nearby Florida. Some people down there swear up and down that he *is* me, though I can promise you he's as human as they come, though perhaps a lot more driven.

Well, let's get this straight. *Are* you Tim Tebow?

No, and I'm not John Wooden, but I bless them both. If it's one thing big-time sports needs right now, it is good role models. I sent them down in times of trouble. Still, you people miss the point. You're still wondering whether a running quarterback can make it in the pros.

Can a running quarterback make it in the pros?

You've got my full attention right now and all you want to know is whether a running quarterback can make it in the pros? Or why it's impossible to only throw up once? It's not impossible, by the way, though I don't expect you to believe me. You've always been a consistent heaver. Are these the questions you want to ask God?

I have loads of questions I'd like to ask God. In fact, I'll list some of them here:

- Did Lee Harvey Oswald act alone?
- What's the over/under on the Super Bowl?
- When is Jesus coming back? I read an article about some gal in Delaware that's had a place set for him since last October.
- When he does come, do we start a new calendar? Will it be like a BC squared or another Y2K?

- Why'd you get rid of Marilyn Monroe so soon?
- Why is it that I am over fifty years old and I'm still growing zits? Don't we ever "graduate" from that?
- What was up with that George W. Bush dude? Were you hacked at us or what?
- Is reincarnation real? If it is and I do come back to earth, does this mean I have to get another date for the prom? Are you serious?

We'll talk about proms and your behavior later, but please continue.

- Why'd you do that to Bill Buckner? I'm a Sox fan when I'm not rooting for the Braves. Seemed kind of mean. And why didn't Steve Prefontaine win a medal in the '72 Olympics in Munich?

I seem to have injected you with too much sport in your blood. Think it was a minor malfunction I incurred when making humans in the sixties. Of course, don't get me started on the sixties. Vietnam was only the half of it!

I could go on, but let's start with relationships, why don't we? I mean, why was I so painfully unsuccessful as a cool high school lad?

Cool? Did you say cool?

Just kidding. But let's take my date with Gail Thompson as a random example. Why couldn't I score—I mean … why couldn't I do well and have fun on my date with her? Why did that night have to turn out a total disaster?

Did you say total disaster? Well, I guess you're right, it was pretty bad. Still, you were and still are a silly boy. All you humans are like this. I send you message after message after message, and yet you allow your egos and your foolish desires—or in this case lustful desires—to

take over, and you block me out *every* time. And then you shake your tiny fists in the air and you blame me! Why, if you'd listened to me, that date would've never happened in the first place!

So you're telling me you were sending me signs?

I'm *always* sending you signs—and again, that's one word and two. They're just not heard. Or you take the meaning and twist it around. Or you pretend you didn't hear—that's my favorite. Or you chalk it up to coincidence. We'll talk more about that word later.

Obviously we have a lot wrong, but let's stay with this example. How were you sending me signs?

By that Bee Gees eight-track tape you were listening to.

Um ... God, I really didn't want the unsuspecting public—even if I don't know them—to know I was listening to the Bee Gees. Couldn't you have said Zeppelin? Or the Who? Or how about the Beatles?

Heh. First of all, you're assuming that people are going to actually read this in the first place. Still, you actually pulled the tape out and put in the Beatles if my memory serves me correctly.

Doesn't your memory always serve you correctly?

Yes, but let's not get off the subject. You ejected that tape and put it underneath your car seat, right next to *An Evening with John Denver.*

God ... Please. I'm trying to save face here.

What? Did your group not think JD was cool? JD sold millions, as did your Bee Gees!

True, but I still couldn't find one single other high school kid that admitted that they liked them. Not *one*! What was up with that? I mean, if those tapes had been found, I'd have been pounded during PE, or at lunch, or anywhere in the hallways by the lockers. Any lockers! My shot at a decent date for homecoming would've been lost forever! And this sounds trivial now, but this was *huge* back then. This was *life*!

So I remember. And yet again, you avoided listening to my message, you ejected the tape, you threw in *Rubber Soul* by the Fab Four, and you proceeded on your date.

And what a horrible date! She couldn't have sat any further away from me. Once, I had to reach behind her and lock her door so she wouldn't fall out. If you remember—well, never mind, of course you remember—back in those days, a lot of your success on a date was determined by how close she sat to you.

Don't worry; I made sure the locks were intact myself.

Thanks. I mean no thanks! It was awful! I felt like I had the plague or something! Why did you waste my time and hers?

Hmm, let's see, waste your time ... this is coming from the same lad who literally got down at the foot of his bed on his knees and begged me for that date. The same lad who promised he'd take out the trash and get along with his brothers if I'd give him that date. The same lad who ...

Okay, I get the point.

Actually, you didn't and probably still don't. You took out the trash once, then went back to your old ways. And you pulled your brother's hair three days later—once during church. To use your own phrase, what's up with that?

Sorry about that.

But don't you see? You beg me and beg me and beg me. Then you blame me and blame me and blame me. If I were human, it'd be one of those moments that would drive me to drink!

What? God drinks!

No, don't worry. God doesn't drink. I have no need. Haven't you heard that saying, "If you're already in Chicago, then you don't need to take a bus to get there"? Never heard that one? Bottom line—I have all I need, including my own self-created buzz when I want one.

A self-created buzz, I like that. But we digress.

Yes, we digress. Let's get back to the norm. First, I send signs. Second, third and fourth, they are not heard but ignored and twisted in your favor.

Couldn't you have at least let me get a kiss at the door? I actually had to lie … I mean, not tell the whole truth to my friends at lunch Monday when they asked.

Let's talk about you and Gail's trip to the door, shall we?

Okay. I actually wrote a poem about it. Want to hear it?

No.

No! Couldn't you be more … I don't know … indirect?

No. Now proceed!

I'd rather not.

No, go ahead. I think your reader might get a kick out of it.

Well, I felt kind of like Kevin on the *Wonder Years* when he was trying to score with Winnie Cooper. Hey, great show by the way!

Thanks, but don't you see how pointless it is to get God off the subject? Now go ahead with your story!

Anyway, the music was playing in my head as we walked side by side to her house. I was gazing at the window—you know, making sure her pop wasn't peering through the shutters. The shutters were closed.

You're welcome.

Oh yeah, thanks for that by the way. He could be mean! I heard rumors that one time that guy—

Ahem.

Sorry. Anyway, she stands and faces me. The music is playing. I'm thinking this is going to be my Kevin Arnold/Winnie Cooper moment. We will embrace, and the fact that she sat so far away, never talked to me, and ordered the most expensive thing on the menu will be long forgotten. She will make up for this and then some. She will realize that actually nerds are cool, football players are overrated and over-muscled, cross country is the next sport of the century, and kids who sit home and write in their diaries over the weekend are, like, the coolest kids ever. And the sexiest!

She was supposed to be thinking like that?

Yes, it's my date! And her steak was expensive! I can dream, can't I? And I actually cleaned my car!

Hence the tapes underneath your car seat.

Ahem yourself. Anyway, there we stand. She is having her moment with Mr. Cool. I'm going to give her the total opportunity to suck face with me. And I am promising in my head not to show off this journal entry to any of my friends. Well, not all of them anyway.

Go ahead. I eagerly await this wonderful ending.

God, I didn't know you could be sarcastic!

Oh, I invented sarcasm. But move along. Your reader is getting antsy for this wonderful ending. Where were we? Date ending, car cleaned, music playing, shutters closed, Gail facing the coolest nerd—I mean kid—ever.

Toe-to-toe, face-to-face, that's where we were. Shutters closed, lights out, nighttime! Problem was, I could swear even the moon was staring down at me. I could hear voices in my head: "Kiss her you geek! Either make this your moment or lie like hell—I mean like heck—about it at school."

And then?

Things got so quiet! I mean, I could actually hear my thoughts. Worse yet, I could swear she heard them too! This never happened to Kevin Arnold. Actually, it did a couple of times, but still, he really was cool. Sort of, anyway.

And so?

And so I pulled her close. I could smell her cologne. (Weird spelling of that word, by the way. What's up with that?) She faced me, eyes closed. I moved in.

And?

And I proceeded to kiss her somewhere on her ear lobe! She turned her head at the last second—gave me the old head fake, she did. I think I kissed her new earrings. And there I was, literally tongue-tied and without a kiss in sight.

Bravo! Bravo!

Not funny!

Come on, it was hilarious! We all got a kick out of that one! And to think, all you had to do was listen to my signs. Listen to yourself. Hear my voice!

I was trying, for God's sake.

Don't blame me for that. You were scoring in your mind, lusting in your heart, and, at the same time, planning on lying to your friends on Monday. Something you still did, by the way.

It wasn't a big lie.

Are you sure about that?

Okay, sorry. Guess it's kind of dumb to lie to God. But you're telling me you could have saved me this trouble?

Trouble? Is growing up trouble? Are valuable learning experiences trouble? Even the process of elimination with the opposite sex, couldn't this be valuable? And okay, I'll admit it, the restaurant was a tad overpriced; you paid a bit too much for that, and she didn't have to order the dessert. She never ate it anyway.

Actually I did.

Yes you did; and then you proceeded to burp in front of her—not a real turn-on, by the way. In getting back to my point, though, sometimes God has to put an exclamation point on his messages. You were literally going to pay for this.

Did you have to make the kids at school start calling me Ear Lobes? It was terribly embarrassing.

What can I tell you; kids can be mean! That's another subject. I'm doing my best. But don't change the subject! You needed to learn to listen!

Okay, thirty-five years later, I'll listen. I'll bite. What was the message? I mean, what was the name of the song you were sending me by the Bee Gees?

Tragedy.

More Relationships

Okay, okay, let's get off of Gail Thompson for a moment.

Don't worry; I took care of that.

What? Was that a crude joke? From God?

First, it wasn't crude. After all, I did—literally—keep you off of Gail Thompson. You're welcome, by the way. I saved you both a lifetime of trouble, disappointment, and anger. Remember the Garth Brooks song "God's Greatest Gifts are Unanswered Prayers"?

Great song.

Thanks!

What? I thought Garth wrote that.

True, and where do you think Garth got the idea? But let me continue. Second, why do people insist that God doesn't have a sense of humor? Who do they think invented humor? Do you think humans invented knock-knock jokes? Do you think the Three Stooges, Robin Williams, and Tim Conway just come up with all their material out of thin air? Or perhaps they—like you all—are being helped?

Sorry, I just have trouble thinking that it was God who kept me off of Gail Thompson. If *my* memory serves me correctly, she did a pretty fine job of that!

You're welcome once again.

Never mind. Let's take some other examples.

Take all the examples you want. I'm just going to keep telling you the same thing over and over and over again.

Well, why aren't your messages more clear?

What could be clearer than the Bee Gees?

Was that another joke? I will contend that once they started using their falsetto voices, they sometimes weren't very clear at all. I will contend that old Bee Gees was better.

Yes. Sorry. Let's try again. What would've been clearer than Led Zeppelin or the Beatles?

Don't you use something besides songs?

I use *everything*! Songs, movies, advertisements, books, random conversations overheard at Dunkin' Donuts, notes passed in class, football coaches' mutterings when you screw up in practice, and even cheerleader chants, for crying out loud! I even tried graffiti on the I-285 interchange!

And I didn't get it?

No, you were daydreaming about another girl, if I remember correctly.

So I didn't get it?

In both cases, no!

God, you're terrible!

And so are you! And I'm tired of getting all the blame! Take responsibility, people—that doesn't just go for you. If I had to talk in human terms, I would tell you all to take some time for silence, shut the *bleep* up, and listen to what your innards tell you!

Your innards?

I'm not talking about your lust for Gail and/or Carole and/or all those other thousands you pined for while you were supposed to be listening in class! I have a voice inside that is *rarely* heard.

God, I promise I tried meditating one time. I really did.

And you lasted 2.8 seconds before you wondered if the Falcons were going to win that day. And whether you were going to Barnes & Noble or not. And how much you were dreading Wednesday's dental appointment. So you did what lots of you do—you gave up! You went back to lust and football and your iPhone and iPod and whatever else I sometimes regret inventing. More on this later.

Let's get back to that iPhone thing. Seriously, will you teach me how to set the alarm?

Ahem!

Sorry, continue.

No, you continue. What else do you want to cover in relationships? Should we discuss your attempt at a marriage? And how you humans have an interesting definition of death doing you part?

God, are you angry with us?

No, I go back to my humor. I laugh to keep from crying. But I digress. What's your question? Shoot.

Are you mad at me for my marriage? I realize I swore until "death do us part" and we only lasted eight-and-a-half years. Am I to be punished or corrected?

I think you've punished yourself quite enough, thank you. And still, there's only one thing you need to know about marriage: the women wear the pants. Period. There are two kinds of men who don't admit to this: divorced ones and liars. And this is coming straight from God himself.

Good to know; too little too late. Was the punishment your doing?

No, it was yours! I'll repeat what I said earlier; you people do an excellent job of punishing yourselves—for years even. Many of you will go to your graves still putting yourselves down, ripping into yourselves, lacking in confidence, and, in the process, driving yourselves to your resting place earlier.

Can we stop doing that?

Yes.

How?

You just stop doing that. Period! Do something else. Think something else. Take a walk. Lift a weight. Shoot some hoops. Call Gail again and ask for another date. It went so well the first time. LOL! (I can get away with text slang, right?) Bake a cake. Or in your case, drive to Chick-fil-A and order a #1 with lemonade. And don't forget to get your refill on the lemonade.

Great lemonade by the way!

Thanks. You didn't think I'd leave a religious fellow like Truett Cathy in the dark did you?

Can we get back to relationships ... or attempts thereof?

Sure, tell me another story. Laughing at you is one of my favorite ways to kill Friday and Saturday nights.

You mean God gets that bored?

Oh no. Think of my office like a Brandsmart with flat-screen TVs everywhere. I can tune in or out whenever I want. I look in on wars, earthquakes, and disasters first, but I always make sure to TIVO you. On a slow day, I call your loved ones around and we have a big chuckle. No booze needed. Again, not that God drinks. Sometimes I watch sports, though I've already discussed how I feel about those who kneel in the end zone after a touchdown.

So your office is like a Brandsmart?

I'm just using references you material-minded humans can understand. It's actually a great deal more complicated—more so than modern remote controls, though those things can be a mess. Programming those things—I blame that on you humans. There is

definitely an easier way. Still, some of you are stubborn and have to make sure you get your way, come hell or high water.

God, you're starting to sound so ... negative.

Negative? I'm just stating facts. I mean, computers are one thing, but you people have taken it *way* too far! Why do you humans like to make things so difficult? You can't even get a human being on the phone when you call places anymore. Did I not make enough humans? Do I need to start over?

You're God; you tell me. Actually, tell me later, I want to talk about relationships some more.

Awesome! I love laughing at you and your relationships. Your dad always swore he taught you better. He's right, by the way. Though he does admire your ability to handle rejection. And you're so good at it!

I suppose I'm supposed to say "Thank you"?

You're welcome, but we digress. Go on, tell me more dating stories. How about your college years? Anything I could've helped you with there? Please say yes, or you're learning less than I thought.

College was just the continuation of Gail Thompson.

"Walked her to the door, tried to kiss her;

She turned her head, by God I missed her!"

Enough with the stupid poems! I'm sorry I ever put those things into your head.

Then why did you?

It was an improvement over what normally went through your head in college.

College—great invention by the way! Congrats!

Sometimes I'm not so sure.

I have a question, though. Why do you have males hitting their sexual peak in the late teens and early twenties while girls don't hit theirs until somewhere in their thirties?

See, I told you I had a good sense of humor. Do you know what college would be like if they were the same? Do you really? Even you would've been pretty successful—nothing personal—and we up here wouldn't have had anything to laugh at. But you're right, college was a great invention, so help me me.

Then why were you not so sure?

I was being flippant again. I needed some invention to keep you people out of the work force for four—or in your case five—more years. I needed something to fill the void. So I invented this party where every now and then a class would break out—though you rarely attended it. You graduated without honors, if my memory serves me correct.

We keep getting off the subject of relationships.

You don't think college life is about relationships? If not, then what years of your life are about them? And let me ask you a question: do you even remember your college years?

I remember it was a time when your reputation was your résumé—whether it was accurate or not.

No, that was truer for females. You guys got off lucky on that score. If there ever was an era of the double standard, it was and always has been college. How did you even know to say that?

Wait ... I'm learning. You put that insight into my head! Otherwise, how else would I have known it? But still, what advice would you give to college kids nowadays?

First, when you walk a girl to the door, put both hands on either side of her head so she can't turn away when you try to kiss her.

No, seriously, what does God say about all this?

It'd be about the same advice I'd give to anybody down there. Start living with gratitude for my sake! Quit complaining. You people down there have everything, and I mean *everything*! You've got the planes, mass communication, iPhones—even though you obviously don't know how to work them—most of you have your health, and I hear *so* much complaining. It's getting so old!

Is God getting upset?

You'd know it if I were upset! With you I could use Mother Nature, bad karma, complicated iPhones, your Braves blowing a lead in the ninth inning, girls faking you out at the door, you name it! Oh the fun I can have with you when I'm upset!

Is that why the Braves never could close the deal in October? Seriously, why did Lonnie Smith not score on that double in Game 7 of the World Series in 1991? And why didn't we take the Yankees with a 2–0 lead in the series in '96? Did we Georgians make you mad about something? Are you mad about Jimmy Carter becoming president? He did okay, didn't he? Or is all this Ty Cobb's fault? He was a great player and all, but the word on the street is he wasn't the nicest human that ever put on a pair of spikes. Or how about Jeff Foxworthy? Is his humor too raunchy for you? Do you not like rednecks? Spill the beans! Are you mad at us southerners?

No, I'm not mad at the Braves, Jimmy Carter, Ty Cobb, Lonnie Smith, Jeff Foxworthy, or southerners in general! Any culture that produces grits and the Peachtree Road Race is okay by me, but more on that later. Or not. Now quit your griping and start being a little more grateful—all you humans could learn this lesson. Count your blessings, not World Series losses. Think of your good fortunes, not miscues on dates or runners left on base in scoring position. Start writing your positives down if you have to, for your own sake!

I used to write things down a lot as a kid. It got me beaten up if I remember correctly. Seriously, I've still got this scar—

I don't want to hear about your scar. You deserved it! Anyway, buy a book, learn to meditate, learn to pray. Oh, and for all of you fast-paced Americans who "don't have the time," use your five minutes of shower time every morning. Let that be your time with God, or Buddha, or whatever you want to call it. And I don't care what you call it, by the way, so quit fighting wars over it! You can call me Gail Thompson if you want to; I don't care! Did you hear that? Now, back to the five minutes. Use those five minutes as your connection to the higher power—the creative energy, if you will. Ask that your connection be strengthened, ask that your decisions be just, ask that you remember the Golden Rule (though more on that later), ask that you go in peace and let others be the same. You people hear this: take that list you recite and those five minutes and make it a daily practice, and the world as you know it will be a *minimum* of fifty percent better in no time!

You just went serious on me! What's up with that?

Sorry about that. In that case, just grab her face, go in gratitude, and get a designated driver! You people scare me sometimes!

God? Scared?

Don't mock me! You're lucky you survived college; you're lucky you're not off on your next assignment, my son. Though again, thanks for the laughs!

You know, the people who lived across from me in my dorm thought Bruce Springsteen could've run for God and probably would've gotten elected. Were you jealous?

You're asking God if he was jealous of Bruce Springsteen?

He was pretty popular, especially with those people from up in New Jersey. You have to admit, "Thunder Road" is a pretty good song. And that double LP—*The River*—he hit it dead on.

Bruce is a wonderful performer—you're welcome—and I'm proud of the talents I gave him.

Well, I just figured you invented jealousy, too, though I'm not really sure what for. I mean, what purpose does it serve? And the same with cockroaches; what good are they? I hear they could survive a nuclear attack, but if we had a nuclear attack, who would want to be greeted by a bunch of cockroaches? What kind of reward is that? Even Stephen King couldn't write an answer for that one!

First off, Stephen King certainly could write for that one—he hit on it closely in *The Stand*, though without the cockroaches. And as for why I invented cockroaches, I must admit—they were a mistake. I was trying to invent another pet—perhaps something a squirrel could play with—and I mixed my chemicals wrong. I didn't want to take

them back, because I wanted to see how it all played out. As it turns out, not too well. We'll discuss your relationship with cockroaches in greater detail later on.

And jealousy?

If used and acted on *properly*, jealousy can be an okay emotion. Please note the word "properly," and don't take this out of context the way you humans do everything else. Anyway, we're going to discuss jealously later in this "manuscript," so hold that thought.

Can we end this chapter now? It's time for a break.

Why, was I striking a nerve?

No, I've just always liked short chapters. Plus, a funny rerun of *The Big Bang Theory* is coming on.

At least you're honest. And one other thing about this sense of humor.

What's that?

Be very glad I've got one—be very glad!

A Ghost in Florida

Let's talk about your nonphysical girlfriend. It intrigues me that you call her that. Speaking of which, why do you call her that?

Because we used to do everything together—we'd hike, go see movies, go to dinner, go to sporting events, hit tennis, go to church. We did everything ... except ... you know.

Would you like to discuss that in greater detail?

Do I want to discuss my lack of a sex life with God? In a word—no!

Why not? You're so helplessly funny! In fact, I'm going to start following you around at parties and put the results on YouTube. Come on; tell us about New Year's Eve. Don't be shy! You've got the floor with God, and you're getting all shy on me.

I promise everything we did was rated G.

True, in spite of all your efforts—though I am using the term "efforts" very loosely. But tell me, didn't you "move in for the kill" one New Year's Eve? I do believe—in fact I know—that you did. And how'd that come out for you? Tell me, I really love your stories sometimes.

I'm so happy I can amuse God.

Okay, I'll set the stage: you're at a New Year's Eve party, counting down the seconds. You've got your eye on your nonphysical girlfriend. There she is, blond hair, smart sweater, smelling all nice, standing in the middle of the room talking to her neighbor. She's talking about real estate in Denver, though you have no way of knowing that. For some reason, you think you can just walk right up. You humans amaze me sometimes, you know? I mean you go from having less than zero confidence to being overconfident with absolutely nothing in between. Haven't you people ever heard of moderation?

I thought moderation was for the fence-sitters of the world who didn't have the guts to make a decision?

Ah, you're quoting from Dan Millman's classic *The Way of the Peaceful Warrior* again. We'll come back to that, or maybe we won't. We're counting down from ten, and here you come. Will you tell us what happened?

Why didn't you send me another sign?

Another sign? How about the fact that she wasn't even talking to you, much less looking at you? You weren't even on her mind. It might have been be a good idea for you to wait until the circumstances were in your favor. I mean, what did you expect her to do—stop in the middle of her real estate brainstorm and plant one on you?

Would've worked for me.

No, it didn't work for you, though it was smooth when you kissed the back of her head and she spilled her wine all over.

Okay, okay, I missed again. We've covered that already. Can we move on?

The question is, when will you move on? You're 0 for 2 here—actually a lot worse—but okay, we'll move on. How about the first time with your wife? Now there's a case where you were actually smooth!

I know! What in the hell—I mean—what happened?

What can I tell you? I created a very tolerant, patient person. Your buffoon style was actually alluring to her. She saw you as a challenge—for a while anyway. Then she moved on and left you to your bottles of antidepressants and your trip to Lancaster without your dog. This led to you being on your knees in Pennsylvania. I believe your exact words were "Dear God, where do I go to surrender?"

I got that question from my dad. You left me depressed for over a year. It was horrible! I had very little will to drink, much less live. Nothing excited me. In fact, I can describe depression in one word: paralyzing. And I mean that mentally and physically. I don't wish that on anyone, even all the girls who "head-faked" me at the door. I wish everyone happiness and peace! Friggin' everyone! It was all I could do to wake up and get out of bed in the morning. In fact, some days I didn't. I just lay there, staring at the walls or the ceiling. I, the social butterfly, would hide when people I knew came my way. I was really starting to get mad at you before I realized that perhaps it was my fault!

Good Lord, you might be learning something after all! Practically everyone blames me during times like this! It's so frustrating! I mean, look at all you learned—besides opening a beer bottle with your left forearm (a horrible habit, by the way). Look how you've changed! Look how self-aware you've become! Don't you see—sometimes you have to flounder. But more on this later. I want to direct your reader's attention to January of 1996.

What was so special about January of 1996? I don't even remember it.

Oh yes you do. You were trying to sleep in your friend's grandmother's trailer in Kissimmee, Florida. It was the wee hours of the morning.

I'm not going to tell that story! I haven't told anybody that story. Ever!

And now is a good time. Do you think God doesn't know all about it? And are you going to tell me you don't have any questions for me about it? Are you really?

Okay, let me start by saying this: I have never, ever, seen a ghost. I wasn't the type in the seventies that saw a UFO every week the way some people did. I've never had visions, hallucinations—heck, I don't even remember my dreams! The only weird thing I can remember is the day it smelled like someone passed gas in my car, I didn't do it, and I was the only one in the car! Weird stuff. Regardless, until I started studying this "God stuff" in the mid-nineties, I considered myself pretty much a five-sensory being.

Please continue, though I can't believe you just brought up passing gas in front of God. Still, go ahead; my interest is piqued.

I was lying in my bed about two in the morning. Couldn't sleep—you know, being in a strange bed and all that. All of a sudden, and I do mean all of a sudden, my shoulders were pinned back to the bed by an unseen body. Scared the ... well, it scared me. It scared me bad. Still pinned to the bed, I heard some panting; in fact, lots of panting. I hate to sound so crude when I'm talking to you, Oh Great One, but it was as if a ghost were molesting me! And a male ghost at that! And I'm not even gay!

Well, you were doing so poorly with humans.

Very funny! But a male ghost? Why couldn't you have at least sent me a female? Regardless, I do have a couple of questions. One, what in the name of you was that, and two, what was the purpose?

What can I tell you; if you're going to have an experience with a spirit, before daylight is a great time! I mean, you weren't busy, were you?

Ahem …

Okay, some people and things even God can't fix; haven't you ever heard that before? Sometimes my spirits get a bit out of control. But let's look at your situation at that time. You were wondering what happens after death—and no, I'm not going to send you back to molest people in trailers. Two, you really were doing poorly in life! You were making less than seven grand a year at the age of thirty-five, your love life, as usually the case with you, had recently been converted to shambles, and you were starting to question things. You've heard the saying "When it rains it pours"? Well, I wanted to speed up your "rock bottom" moment and get you going again. If I recall—and I do—you actually had a good laugh about it when you got back to Atlanta. There you were, snowed in and eating your ramen noodles. The roaches were all asleep in your cabinets, bedded for the night. Your place was a mess. And you started laughing—out loud—at your plight, as you should have. Laughter is good; humor is good. But still, let me continue, because here is the kicker. You still, even to this day, question whether anything happens after this life even though I sent you solid proof! Yet still you question! How much more clearly could I have made that experience?

Sorry, Oh Lord, but I am officially mad all over again. My life, as you admitted, was going poorly; basically it was in shambles. And you, you send me a *male* ghost to molest me while I'm in the sack minding my own business. How can I, or how did I, ever get over this? I think I repressed that one. Thanks, by the way, for bringing it back up!

Well, we talked earlier about signs, though, did we not? Remember the Bee Gees tapes? Songs, as you now know, don't work very well with you. I had to shake you up a bit—literally. And I did!

I've kept that secret for so long I'd almost forgotten it happened. I mean, who would I tell besides my two readers right now? I do remember my poor self-esteem after it happened: going to work at my below-minimum-wage position, having been recently dumped by a twenty-five-year-old and less recently raped by a male ghost, having no gas in my car and no power at home—and *Two and a Half Men* hadn't been invented yet. What was a human to do?

Give yourself credit every now and then. You plodded forward. You got out of bed in the morning, you quit embalming yourself with beers as much, and you got a new job. Do you realize it was only five months later when you met your wife?

But did you have to rape me with a male ghost? I'm going to keep asking you that!

What can I tell you; the normal signs don't work with you. You can be a bit self-absorbed. Most of you are. You're hard to reach and to teach. So I sent my most morally loose spirit and told him to have at it! Gave you a night to remember, even though you never actually got to see it. I hate to break the news to you, though, but he wasn't very impressed.

I don't care! And I was all freaked out, and I couldn't tell another living soul. I just had to keep it in and act like nothing happened. Just another day in the life when attacked by a ghost—no big deal! But let's go back to this life after death thing—does this mean my daddy is okay?

See, there you go again. How about you tell the story of what happened between you and your daddy *after* he died. Spare nothing.

Just tell the story. Not only am I listening, but I also helped him send the message.

Okay, get the picture: my dad was on his deathbed, about to pass away from cancer. He was wearing a UGA T-shirt that read "Jawja." It said that because, being from the north, that's the way he pronounced Georgia. He died with that shirt on; for all I know he was cremated in it. Anyway, fast forward two weeks later. I had just self-published a novel entitled *Alumni Hall, Room 34.* To give it a quick book review, it blew. Still, that's not the point. The point is, I was doing a book signing—or, as I started calling them, a book sitting—at one of the local malls. Not only did I sell nothing, but not a living soul came anywhere near me. I just sat there for two hours twiddling my thumbs.

Keep going. This is where I— or shall I say your father—stepped in.

I was driving home, all depressed. I was starting to question events, life, and who invented talcum powder. *Who am I to write a book anyway?* I thought. *I mean, why not just live out my days as normal as I can and just carry forward.*

And?

And at that *very* moment I was having these thoughts, a car cut across two lanes of traffic, forcing me to hit my brakes. The license plate read "Jawja."

Your reaction?

I started laughing! Goose bumps shot up my arms.

And how did you interpret this?

I interpreted it as a message from my father. He was telling me to hang in there, keep going, and not give up. He was patting me on the back for my effort and telling me not to quit.

You know what?

What?

That's exactly what you were supposed to be thinking. I, or shall I say we, finally sent a message to you that was received, heard, and understood. Game, set, match, as you like to say. I even gave your dear old dad a high-five for that; we both knew we'd made a clear connection—finally! But continue. You have another tale for us. Talk about your experience at the cemetery.

Okay, it was our first Christmas without Dad. I had this all planned out: I was going for a four-mile run that was going to end at his grave. Then I was going to sit all dejected at the foot of his grave—you know, the way the Royals' shortstop Freddie Patek did in the dugout after the playoffs when he hit into a double play for the final two outs, allowing his team to fall to the mighty Yanks back in the seventies.

You're perhaps the only human that remembers that, but go ahead.

So there I sit, feeling all sorry for myself, head in hands, Georgia clay creeping into my running shorts, shoes, and veins and—

And then?

And then, even though it was a perfectly calm day, a small tree branch fell and dropped onto my head.

Please continue.

And then a thought popped into my head as clearly as any ever did.

And what was that thought?

"If you're sitting here now feeling sorry for yourself, then you're missing the whole point. Get your butt up, dust yourself off, go home, and take care of your mom, your brothers, your wife, and your dog. Now go!"

And what did you do?

I started laughing again. But I got up and went.

Are you starting to see a point here? And yet you still question me even after all of these things. Do you think all of this was a coincidence—your late-night friend, the car plate, the tree branch? Do you get it yet, or do I need to send you back to another trailer in Florida?

I get it, I get it!

Sadly, I'm not sure you do, but I hear you.

Signs

So what are you up to this weekend?

Well, tonight I'm going to drink some two-buck-Chuck wine and talk to God. I never thought I'd say that with a straight face. Tomorrow I was supposed to go hiking in the North Georgia Mountains with a woman, but she stood me up.

Oh dear, more love life woes!

No! Anyway, I'll probably run at the river, watch my school compete in a wrestling tournament, and then hit a local tavern Saturday night. Sunday I'm playing league tennis at Horseshoe Bend in Roswell. I'm playing mixed doubles with my friend Monika. After that, it's probably a nasty TV dinner or some cereal, a little SportsCenter, some reruns of *How I Met Your Mother*, and off to sleep.

Might I make a suggestion?

Sure, you're God. You can pretty much do whatever you want.

Might I suggest you take me with you during all of this? You admitted you planned on talking to me tonight, but when after that?

You wait until Sunday during church—oops, you're not going to church. When were you going to visit again?

Take you with me! You want to hang out in some of the places I hang out in? Really? Somehow I just can't picture introducing God to a cocktail waitress. It just sounds … wrong!

You don't think I love cocktail waitresses? There are several out there you'd do more than fine to end up with. You've actually had thoughts in your conniving skull about several if I'm not mistaken— and we've already covered that I'm not. So sure, introduce me to your favorite one. Take me to tennis Sunday. Take your notepad with you and write down your questions. Well, in your case, some of your questions anyway.

How about this—I take you on a day-in-the-life and then you tell me what signs I missed? I feel like this is high school baseball all over again. I'm on first (how I got there I'll never know!), and the coach is using every sign in the book trying to get me to steal second. Me, I'm so glad to be on first I don't want to take a chance on getting out at second. So I'm just looking off in the stands to make sure as *many* people as possible see me there in all my glory. Boy would my coach get mad!

May I tell you a secret?

Cool, secrets from God … go ahead!

I *am* that coach sending signs. And you, as well as most of you humans, keep missing them. Sign number one—when a woman isn't even looking at you, don't walk up and try to plant one on her. That *does not* work. Ever!

Very funny!

Who's being funny? You need help! I've got a lot of things going on right now, and I'm not sure what's to be done about you. Hold on a second.

Another flood?

No, somebody just slam dunked in Wisconsin, and he wants me to acknowledge it. You athletes are simply killing me! It wasn't even that great a dunk. The pass was much better, but the point guard's not signaling to me at all. You people need to learn who to give the proper credit to. Maybe that can be your job.

You think I can handle it?

Doubtful, but let's start with football. Make it a fifteen-yard penalty every time somebody takes off his helmet in the end zone after a touchdown. Do they not think I know what they look like? Let me quote from one of your great coaches—Lou Holtz—who I sent your way in the twentieth century: "It's okay to take off your helmet after a good play, as long as you take off your helmet after a bad one." Sounds good to me!

We're back to Herschel Walker again.

Yes, a *perfect* example of what to do after making a good run. Simply act like you do it all the time, hand the ball to the ref, and then get your butt off the field! It really couldn't be simpler! What is it with you humans? Have you ever seen a teacher breakdance after delivering a good lecture or driving home a good point? Now *there's* a profession that deserves to showboat every now and then. That's why I don't make teachers wear helmets, by the way.

You thought of making teachers wear helmets?

No, I *want* people to know what they look like! I *want* you to remember them. Remember them, listen to them, emulate them, respect them, appreciate them. Add them to your gratitude list, and thank them in your five minutes.

Sorry to laugh at you; I'm just trying to picture my seventy-year-old Latin teacher with a football helmet on, breakdancing in front of the room. Might've made the class a tad more interesting. The best sleep I ever got during four years of high school was during Latin class. To quote from Jack Nicholson, "I'd rather have stuck needles in my eyes."

I do believe your grade reflected that attitude. Those were some of the few times you talked to me during those years—every time that teacher started passing out one of her tests.

Did you listen?

Let's just say I gave you the same respect I give those athletes for sending me signals after they do something they're paid to do in the first place. But let's go back to you and your weekend plans. If I'm not mistaken—*ahem*—I do believe you have something to share with your readers.

I do.

Yes, let's start with Friday afternoon after school. Tell me about your mood when driving home and tell me why you felt that way.

Well, I was depressed because this manuscript was at a dead end. I mean, I wrote twenty pages without catching a breath, but then I kept getting stuck.

Go on. What'd you do next?

I did what millions of Americans do when they're bored at home with nothing to do, nobody to go out with, and no good ideas flooding my mind—I got on Facebook!

And what did you find there?

Mostly crap. I mean, what is it with these people that insist on telling you that they're about to go to the mall or about to clip their fingernails. They're my friends and all, but who cares? Some people even write about what they're having for dinner! Do I care? I don't even know what I'm having for dinner; can't remember what I had for lunch.

You're avoiding the subject. What did you see there that stuck out at you?

Well, at the bottom of my Home page was a note from Deepak Chopra, who many know is a noted speaker, author, and doctor, and who is, in my humble opinion, one of the most intelligent humans on this planet.

I agree; now what did the note say.

It said, and I paraphrase, "Be persistent! And don't allow old ways of thinking to creep in!"

What did this mean to you?

I felt he was talking to me! I do that *all* the time. I begin a project, I get a couple pages in, and then I lose both confidence and steam, and I don't know which goes first. I start thinking in my old ways: *Who am I to do this? Who cares what I'm thinking? Why don't I just go to school, retire at seventy-five, and then ride off into the great beyond?*

Continue with your story.

I kept repeating Deepak's message to myself over and over before I went to sleep. Still, I woke up depressed again. Maybe that was due to the three glasses of wine, but still, nothing had come to me. But I would *not* let my old ways of thinking in. *Never.*

So you got up and went to Dunkin' Donuts—something even God can't keep you from doing, by the way.

Sure, I got my coffee and then went for a run at the river. I usually go to the Chattahoochee about three to five times per week. Great invention, by the way!

Thanks, it was—both the running and the river.

While I was running, it was as if the floodgates opened. My mind became clear, ideas started popping in, I got "unstuck," and I couldn't wait to get back to my desk at school—even though it was a Saturday. It was awesome!

Now, allow me to take over. And if your readers never get another word of this manuscript, I want them to get this: When you exercise your own uniqueness and begin doing the things you are supposed to be doing, I always (one word and two) lend a hand. You will get the "lucky breaks," the "chance encounters," the "coincidences," the "idea that just popped in." This is *always* the way in which I work! Now, my question to you is, are you going to go back to your old ways of thinking, or are you at least going to consider that I work through each and every one of you if and when you tune in—if and when you exercise who you really are? Or are you going to just think, "Hmm, I was jogging along one day and I finally got a good idea! Duh, where'd that come from?"

Is God getting frustrated? And you keep changing gears—funny to smart guy to serious.

As your dad used to say, "Keep 'em guessing!

I would say you're pretty good at that. Are you frustrated?

With you, you bet your life I am! Now get it! You were jogging (something that works well with you mentally and physically, by the way) and you were exercising your unique idea (another thing I gave you). You were doing what you were supposed to be doing and then *wham*, you got unstuck. *Please* don't dismiss this as another strange coincidence. There are *no* such things as coincidences. They are put out there!

Okay, you said earlier you were going to say more about coincidences.

I will. People have the definition of "coincidence" wrong down there on earth. If two angles coincide, they actually go together. So why in the world do you people use the word coincidence to refer to two unrelated things fitting together? As you would say, what's up with that?

Now, can we go back to being wise guys? I'm starting to lose my reputation. Still, it is hard for me to even *imagine* a God that would even want to work with or through someone like me. In fact, I almost titled this manuscript *Irreverent Conversations with God*.

And I'll tell you what I told author Neale Donald Walsch: It should've been called *Wonderfully Irreverent Conversations with God*. Again, where do these ideas come from?

But I have been all things unholy times fifty-seven—or more! I can't imagine taking you with me to some of my hangouts, much less inside the filth that masquerades as my mind! In fact, just this past Christmas, I wrote a Christmas card so irreverent—I can't even believe I sent it out. You would've shot me!

No I wouldn't! Why do people insist that I have to be serious and that you have to be dressed to the nines before you can even talk to me? I love humor. But please don't put that card in here; the world is in no way ready for that yet. Just keep that among the sixty or so friends you have in your e-mail chain.

Whew! I thought you were going to make me share it.

Not on your life or mine. I'm not sure if you're ahead of your time or behind it, but the world is definitely only ready for you in small doses. Relax; I'll take some of that blame. Now let me continue, and then I'll allow you to be a smart aleck again. You can talk humorously to me; you can even write a book entitled *Funny Conversations with God* if you want to. I'm not going to punish you, so get over it! Now, let's continue.

Oh Great One, can I ask you something?

Of course. I thought that was the point of all this. Shoot.

Why don't you get on Facebook?

Ahem.

Seriously, what better way to reach all of us knuckleheads than to get on Facebook! When I was snowed in last week, I'd have loved to chat with you that way—would've saved you a phone call.

Why is it so important that I get on Facebook?

Well, I'd love to see your profile picture for starters. Whatever do you look like? And what would you put under "birth date" or "education"? I'm curious. You should consider it! Or are you scared people wouldn't friend you? I promise I would.

Good to know if I went on Facebook I'd have a friend. Sadly, many people wouldn't because they're too scared of me … or they'd consider it blasphemy … or they'd say I was the devil.

You mean people don't think God could get on Facebook? I could teach you, you know. It's not that hard. You just open up your laptop, go online and—

Ahem.

Sorry, I guess I don't have to tell God how to go online. You'd be an instant hit! I mean, I've got over four hundred friends, but you'd eclipse that in no time. Plus, you could give me good insight on who to hide from my home page, who to be friends with, who to ignore when they chime in to chat. You could be a real timesaver! I don't want to keep reading from those people who insist I care what they're eating and where they're going!

That's just what you need—more free time on your hands. I've already taken away your wife, you have no kids, you've already seen every episode of *Two and a Half Men*, we've already discussed *Columbo*, and now you're talking about more free time! Most people would kill for your schedule!

And that's where you could come in on Facebook. I'd totally read your posts. They'd be way better than those nail-clippers that get on there. I mean, I read Deepak's quote, and you're probably smarter than he is. Aren't you?

You've asked me if I'm Tim Tebow, and now you're asking if I'm smarter than Deepak Chopra? Sometimes you really ask for it, you know that?

But that's why you love me! Right? That's my uniqueness and my boldness! I trust the Bible, I have no desire to pick apart religions, and I respect everyone's right to believe what they want to believe; all I want to do is joke around with you and ask you whether Lee Harvey Oswald acted alone or not.

And why did I kill off Marilyn Monroe, why did I do that to Bill Buckner, why was Buddha a bit girth-challenged, why—

Okay, sorry about that.

Don't be sorry; some of these are legitimate questions. First off, you people down there lay off of Bill Buckner! Do you realize—and many don't—that he was a .289 lifetime hitter? That's a solid stat for those who don't know baseball. He hit 174 career homers ... wait ... stats are boring, so I'll say no more. Now please, continue.

Speaking of legitimate questions, would you "defriend" me if I sinned?

I'm going to let you answer that question yourself. Have I ever "defriended" you? And trust me, you *have* sinned!

Did you have to put an exclamation point after that? I'm trying. After all, to quote from one of my old tennis players, "I'm only cheating myself, and if I can deal with it, then you should be able to."

Are you being smart with God?

No, but boy was he being smart with me!

Well, did you punish him?

No, I bent over laughing! No player has ever been so ... honest ... with me before. How do you respond to that?

I laughed myself, actually; it was your player, Brian, expressing his own special uniqueness. He's lucky he had you as a coach. A lot of coaches out there would've busted his chops for that one.

Perhaps, but can I digress for a second?

Good grief! Have you ever been tested for ADD?

Certainly.

And?

The doctor told me I was so far off the charts that my *goal* was to get back to ADD!

Your doctor was a funny and an accurate man. Now go ahead. Digress.

My iPod got stolen out of my car last Tuesday morning. What are you going to do about it?

I've already done something about it.

You mean you caught the guy? Who was it?

No, I didn't catch him. I made you start locking your car, granite head! You don't leave a car unlocked in Atlanta, Georgia; it's just not done. People come by all the time, look in your windows, see something they like, pound out the window, and poof, they're gone. You lost a computer the same way three years ago. Did you learn from it? No, you started making it *easier* on them; you started leaving your car *unlocked*. I'd love to hear the "logic" on that one. And taking it further, after a robbery like your most recent one, many of you down there would shake your fists and blame me!

So you're not going to tell me who did it? Do you know who did it?

You're asking God if he knows who stole your iPod? I think I am going to get on Facebook. I'm going to start recording some of your questions for all to see. Do I know how to set the alarm on an iPhone? Do I know who stole your iPod? Why didn't I send you a sign before you tried to play tonsil hockey with Gail Thompson? Of all the questions you could and should ask, *these* are the things you want to know?

I read somewhere to "ask and ye shall receive."

You read that the last time you went to church. How long ago was that? Five years? And you only went because you thought your date was hot. Now, lock your car, take your valuables inside or put them in the trunk, use your common sense, and quit trying to get me to sign up for Facebook! I have no time!

But you have to be good at splitting your attention! I mean, one Sunday I saw two different guys kneeling in the end zone calling your name, and they were in two different states! If you can listen to both of them, answer prayers, give guidance, make calls on your new phone and listen to all of us humans complain all the time, surely you've got at least time for a cameo! Most of us would *love* to hear from you. And again, I *promise* I would be your friend.

You promise?

Is God suffering from a confidence problem?

No, I'm leaving that one with you. I was just being flip. Now let's get back to your weekend. You went out Saturday night, and you lusted over a cocktail waitress about half your age.

Ahem ... God!

Sorry for being so honest. Let me rephrase: You went out and had a casual, innocent conversation with a cocktail waitress that you totally enjoy being friends with … no ulterior motives whatsoever. You were very impressed at how good of shape she's in. You started to make a comment about this, but I diverted your attention; I made you drop your glasses on the floor. You're welcome, by the way; you were about to really screw up—again!

Okay, can we skip the cocktail waitress?

Oh, I'll see to it, and you're welcome once again. Now, let's move ahead. Let's continue with your weekend. Pick it up on Sunday morning.

Well, I had an extra cup of coffee at my spot; you know, something about painful head conditions.

We can skip that part. Move ahead.

Okay, I went off to my office to do some work. I collected basketball, wrestling, and swimming scores from the weekend and wrote them up for my job. After that, I got three or four pages written on this manuscript, which I consider a good day.

And then?

I went running in the gym. It was too cold to go out—around thirty-five degrees or so—so I did the boring run around and around the top of the gym. Boring, but I got my three miles in.

And what happened during the run?

Well, our girls' golf coach came in—I guess to do some work of her own. I was in the middle of my workout when she yelled across the gym,

"Keep going!" Now, I'm not an idiot (I don't think), and I knew she was talking about my running. But I took it as something more holistic than that—if that's the proper word. I took it to mean "Keep going with your work, keep going with your project, keep going with your life." After all, it's fast approaching my five-year divorce-aversary—something that's been on my mind. Anyway, her encouragement reminded me of the Deepak quote again, and how not to let the old ways of thinking creep in. What a great coincidence!

Ahem!

Just kidding. I know there are no such things. Your message was sent and received!

And do you know how rare that is? For you humans to keep your minds focused and clear enough for that to happen? Do you know how happy that makes me? Do you know how well you people would be doing if you had Bill Buckner's .289 lifetime average as far as messages received? Now, here's where I want you to give yourself some credit, and don't start apologizing for it. You made the decision to carry me with you this weekend. I sent you a sign. You got it. Congratulations!

What now?

What did the sign say—keep going! Take me to work tomorrow; take me to your meetings. Oops, never mind, you never go to meetings. Good for you, by the way, and let *me* know how you managed that one. I might have you start giving a class—some type of orientation on *The Power of Avoiding Meetings.*

So you don't like meetings either?

Let's go back to that .289 number again—that's about the percentage of the ones that are truly effective. Actually, the number

is a good deal lower than that, but that's another topic for another time. But continue; the weekend's not over. And I'm not going to let you off the hook about your divorce-aversary; that's something we should address.

Later is as good a time as any.

There you go again, but go ahead. Move on. Literally. But wait— let me be as ADD as you for a second. You need yoga!

Me, yoga?

Come on, Bee Gees boy! Is yoga not macho enough for you? You are by far the tightest marathon runner I've ever created, plus you need the spiritual side. It's … holistic, to use the word you threw out a while ago. What a coincidence you should use that word—ha ha. Anyway, write it down somewhere. Spread the word. It would help even the most macho of the football players down there.

You think so?

Sure. It would even make it easier on them when they bow to me in the end zone—their joints wouldn't creak as much. Yoga, humans— just try it. Now, go ahead with your weekend. I'm as ready for you as I can get—I think.

Okay, so I was off to Horseshoe Bend to play my tennis match. On the car radio, Elton John's "I'm Still Standing" played, which I thought was an exclamation point on your earlier sign.

Good call; continue.

Of course, the station followed that with Bananarama, and I turned it. What's up with Bananarama?

Hey, don't rip on Bananarama! They exercised their gifts and their uniqueness. The majority of you people down there would be good to follow suit.

Well, what was up with the eighties in general as far as music? I mean, what other decade has a four-hour special on one-hit wonders? It was messed up as far as music is concerned.

I'd prefer to think it was a decade where more people than ever before got to exercise their vocal and musical gifts. See, you're so negative sometimes. You need to work on that. But go ahead.

Well, my partner—Monika—and I won our match 6–0, 4–6, 6–2, and then—

Stop right there!

What for?

I want to make something clear. For some reason, when it comes to sports, a lot of you humans totally check out as far as your common sense is concerned. I want to make sure you and both your readers understand that you didn't win because I was "on your and Monika's side." In fact, I was just as much on your opponents'—Richard and Harriet's—side as I was yours. I want to be *very* clear on that. You'd be surprised how many of you go into sports claiming I'm on your side. What a crock!

You sound frustrated again. But in moving on, there's nothing much else to report. It was a nice day for tennis, though I've had mixed thoughts on the game over the years.

Overall a good game; not that much work needs to be done with it.

So tell me your thoughts. Wooden rackets or the new, powerful ones? Grass or clay? Nadal or Federer? What's your deal?

My only problem with tennis is the "quiet please."

The "quiet please"?

Think of it this way: a quarterback stands over center with the crowd screaming and yelling, the opposing defense yelling things about his mother, and linemen waiting to tear his head off. All this time, he is expected to shut out all the noise, read the opposing defense, change the play at the line of scrimmage, communicate this to his teammates, and then, after all this, successfully execute the play with all the noise going on.

So?

So let's take another example from another sport. Same crowd— let's reduce it to 45,000 since baseball stadiums are smaller. The catcher—he has to watch the base runners, know the strengths and weaknesses of his pitcher, know what pitch to call in what situation, and position his fielders, and he has to repeat the process after every pitch. With, by the way, crowd noise in the background.

Again, so?

So why can't a tennis player serve a ball when a spectator in Row 5 is standing up? I mean, to quote from you again, what's up with that? Isn't concentration a part of being an athlete? I mean, I also could've talked about a point guard in basketball or used several other examples, but again, what's the deal?

Never thought of it like that.

Neither have most tennis players. Tell them to go to a tennis match at the University of Georgia. That's at least *close* to what it should be. Otherwise, I love the game. After all, any game with love in the score has to be okay with God, right?

I agree. Now, on a personal note, do you think I should start playing again as much as I used to?

No, I think you should go back to taking your meds before somebody gets hurt. Now finish off your weekend.

Well, there's not much left to report. I went home and watched football, wrote up the tennis match, showered, and tried to sleep.

You "wrote up" tennis?

Yes, that's another good idea you gave me! Want to see it?

You're going to blame me for that? There you go again.

What?

Just kidding. Whatever floats your boat; if you like writing about things, go for it. At least it keeps you off of cocktail waitresses. Now, before you insert that thing in here, *please* clean it up a bit. You know what they say in speech class: know your audience. Ahem!

Okay, let me find it. Here it is.

Acers Come from Behind for 3–2 Win
Drop Horseshoe Bend for Second Win in a Row

With Katie's dog—Spencer—on hand, Amir's Acers faltered early but came from behind for an exciting, baby-throwing, 3–2 win over Horseshoe Bend in Roswell Sunday. This marked the second straight win for our heroes, running their point total to eight.

When asked for a comment, Spencer—who also acts as the team's general manager—simply hiked up his leg and left the facility. Memos are sure to follow.

Back to the courts, the match came down to our #5s, as Mike Reiter and Abby Brunelle steamrolled their opponents for a 6–0 first-set win in front of all five screaming Acers fans.

Opening up a 5–3 second-set lead, Horseshoe fought back and got ahead 6–5 before Brunelle-Reiter edged out a 7–5 win in the tiebreaker.

Beer, champagne, and overall bedlam followed.

"Today we just didn't stink," Brunelle didn't say afterward. "We played well when we had to."

The match started out all Horseshoe, as their #1 team consisted of a right-handed version of Martina Navratilova and a guy who wasn't so bad his self. They fought off Katie Soskin and Stephen Wells for a 7–5, 6–3 victory.

"I hit the softest ball on that court," Wells would say later.

Horseshoe didn't exactly drop off at #2, where our beloved hero and captain, Melissa Amir Smith, and her husband, Brandon, went down 6–2, 6–2.

"Rats," Brandon said. "Maybe next time!"

The bleeding stopped right there, however, as the Acers picked up wins at both #3 and #4 to keep the match alive. At #3, Dunn and Monika won the first set in 7.2 seconds by a 6–0 margin before temporarily going to their "dark places" and dropping a 6–4 second set. After taking a quick break, making adjustments, and getting more aggressive, the duo coasted to a 6–2 third-set win.

At #4, our competitive warriors—Jansen and Leslie Stamps—again left no doubt. After squeaking out a 6–4 set, they coasted for a 6–2 win in the second to put all the pressure on Mike and Abby.

"Jansen was dominating today," Leslie said afterward. For the record, she *really* did say that—I promise!

From there, Abby and Mike heroically responded, and that was pretty much that.

Looking ahead: Next Sunday is another road match. The team bus leaves at 11:48 a.m. for Old Towne, where we will probably be playing on the clay. Hopefully Spencer will be there, though he prefers hiking his leg on hard courts as opposed to the dirt. Still, we'll try to make him proud. We are probably in the middle of the pack as far as the standings. We're used to that; this is like our fourth season at A1, and we are *always* in the middle of the pack. Diane Morone, phone home. The Horseshoe people were nice, but our food is just as good as theirs. I'm just saying.

Until next time,

Dunn
#5 player who played #3
Team Scribe and Idiot
Nerd

"Have you ever noticed that the person telling you to calm down is usually the same person that made you mad in the first place?"

—Garrison Keillor, I think

By the way, thanks for cleaning that up! Like I say, this world isn't totally ready for you yet. But finish up; I believe you had something else to ask me.

I do, actually; it came to me while I was taking my shower.

Ahem. Do we really want to know this?

Yes, it's just a question. Here goes: why is it that I could go out to a tennis match today, see someone I haven't seen in over twenty years, and totally remember his name and everything about him, and yet find myself standing in the shower, not even able to remember if I've washed my hair. What's up with that?

What can I tell you? Some questions even God can't answer.

God Enters the School System

You know I can't hang around with you Monday through Friday, don't you?

Why not? I enjoyed having you around over the weekend. Don't leave me now; I'm at work. I need you more than ever! I loved the signs you sent me; I'm actually starting to look for them and seek them out. Believe it or not, I'm almost sort of paying attention!

Thank you, and good for you. The problem, however, is that you work at a school. God isn't allowed in schools anymore!

Good Lord!

Thank you.

No, I mean, good Lord, you're right! I forgot about that. Come join me anyway. Not having you in our school system is a crock! Give me some time; I'll devise some way to sneak you in my school.

Don't get in trouble with your boss!

Boss—did you say boss—as in singular? I've got about ten bosses.

You need about ten bosses!

Point taken, but I'm going to work on this! Wouldn't that be a hoot—God back inside the gates of a school in America! We could put that on CNN for sure!

Are you sure you'd watch that over Braves baseball or all those sitcoms you spend so much "quality" time watching?

I realize that I have much less than a .289 batting average, but you can count on me! You're on second base, and I'm bringing you home!

Well, okay, but don't tell anybody! I mean, if I get in trouble, I'll expect you to put up for me. Also, I don't want to get you fired; you may be putting your job at risk by letting me get my foot back in the door.

If you can't risk something for God, then who can you risk something for? No, this is going to happen. Not only that, but I'm also subbing some this week, and I'm actually going to take you *inside* the classroom again! How's that sound? You can actually get reacquainted with our educational system.

Wow, I'm getting all teary eyed.

Is God being sarcastic?

You better believe I am. I need to be brought into your classrooms now more than ever. It's ironic that just when I am needed most, I am being pushed away. So yes, I'll accept your invitation. If I'm carded at the door, I probably won't be admitted, though, so you'll have to be my official eyes and ears. You're a reporter; send me a report or two—an official memo, if you will—and keep me informed. I miss school—it was always so fun for me.

Now you're getting nostalgic.

Who would have thought? I can understand the "powers that be" trying to keep drugs and guns out of our schools, but I never thought I'd see the day when I had to go. So all during this manuscript, I expect reports from you about our kids. What do they say? How are they? What are they thinking? What are their thoughts, wishes, goals? It makes me sad to hear all those bells ringing from afar and not being allowed in. Though I've enjoyed our little tongue-in-cheek bantering throughout, I weep in frustration sometimes at what you humans have done to me. So could you please let me go in with you? I promise I'll be nice—I will raise my hand at the appropriate time, will speak only when spoken to, will not pick on the other kids. This could actually be fun. And trust me on this: I cannot thank you enough for your invitation. I now weep in happiness.

For God's sake, let the school bells ring.

You know, I couldn't have said that much better myself.

May I remind you of something that happened to me back in the sixties, back when you could get in the doors without an ID? We said the Pledge of Allegiance back then—put our hands over our hearts, prayed, and the whole nine yards.

Yes, I remember. Tell me the story, though, I love hearing stories about our kids.

Well, I was in first grade and I was acting up. I know this is hard for you to imagine. My best friend was named Don Gilbert—he was a great student, but unfortunately for him, I often took him down to my level. Anyway, one day I was talking out of turn, throwing spitballs, and basically wreaking general havoc across our wonderful classroom.

And?

And Miss Thornton called me up to the blackboard, drew a circle on it, and made me stick my nose in it.

Good for her.

Exactly. Well, to make her point, she turned to the classroom and said in a stern voice, "Now, does anybody want to join him?" Don couldn't raise his hand fast enough. "I do! I do!" And with that, my buddy Don came up and joined me.

Cute story, and I remember it. Now fast forward for me to this decade and keep the reports coming. I hear rumors about our educational system, but I need more. You're my official James Bond.

No, I'm not going to be your James Bond! I'm going to sneak you in. I've actually got a foolproof plan. Okay, it's not as good as the Tom Cruise *Mission Impossible* scene—you know, the one where he's literally hanging by a cord in the gallery. Beads of sweat line his face, and if one bead hits the ground, an alarm goes off and he is screwed. It's not that good, but still, I think I've got it.

Tell me; how are we going to pull this off? Do tell.

I'm going to sneak you in through our janitor's broom closet. It's not fancy, like I said, but I think it can happen. Get the picture: people are used to seeing me roam the halls at school—I'm the equivalent of background noise from I-285: You hear it always, but it's such a normal sound that you eventually tune it all out. Same with me; it'll just be another day at school with me pacing the hallways and the classrooms. When nobody's looking, I'll go into the closet and leave the back door open. You can just come on in, though I would suggest you wear the school uniform.

The school uniform?

Oh yes, God, you're going to have to dress like a janitor. You'll need khaki pants, a collared shirt, and some tennis shoes. Wear a hat—you'll need to pull it down low when key people come by. Remember, no smoking!

Ahem, I think I knew that, thank you very much. I put that in place myself.

Okay, we'll do this backward. You're invited to come in tomorrow, and this time I'll expect a full report from you. I'll ask how your day went when the day is done, and I'll take notes. That makes me much more comfortable than having me screwing up and you critiquing me. I'd rather just take notes.

You mean, sort of like in a classroom?

Yes, the pun was intended.

(Fast forward to Tuesday morning. Said door has been propped open, and God has spent the entire day in our school. Oddly, he never left the sophomore hallway—that's where the broom closet is located. Instead, he swept, cleaned off lockers, fixed broken lockers, and swept some more. The following is his report.)

Dear me what a beautiful day!

There's more to our school than just the one hallway, you know. We've got a cafeteria, a gym, a preschool, a lower school, a middle school, and three more halls in the upper school.

Good to know. I had everything I needed, however, right where I stood.

Would you care to tell me about it?

Boy, would I ever! You have to help me get started first.

How?

**Briefly tell the story of why you could never walk your dog—
Jasper—at the Chattahoochee River.**

What's that got to do with anything?

**Everything actually—now go. Time is short. Someone in the
Dominican League has a no-hitter going, and he's talking to me.**

Okay, I took Jasper to the river once. It was a born-again disaster! He
wanted to sniff everything … and everybody. Every single runner that came
in, every walker that strolled by, every bird watcher that cruised past, every
cyclist that pedaled on—he wanted some of everybody. The same with the
bushes and the plants—he wanted to pee on all of them. It was sensory
overload times twelve! I got frustrated with him at the quarter-mile point,
turned around and took him home. Funny thing was, he was asleep in his
seat in the car before we ever got out of the river parking lot. That was odd;
usually in a car he would paw at the window whenever another car would
pass us going the other way. I always wondered about that—I mean, what
was he going to do when and if he caught the other car? It always made me
laugh. But anyway, he was sound asleep practically before I put the car in
drive. It was *so* cute. Now, what does that story have to do with anything?

**Two words that you hit on—*sensory overload*. Or, to borrow
your quote from earlier—sensory overload times twelve. That was
me right when I set foot in the broom closet. The ammonia smell—it
was the aroma of old gymnasium hardwood floors, and my mind
went cruising. In fact, it went on overdrive so hard I had to double
over—almost in pain. People have this vision of me as being stoic and**

unfeeling—what a crock! I feel *everything*! I *am* everything. I couldn't even grab my broom—I was clutching my knees, smelling that acrid smell, my mind cruising off in time. I guess the first story that came up that happened on your very gym floor was from years ago; it involved a ninth grader named Billy Quinn.

Who in the world was that?

It doesn't matter, but here's the story: Fifteen people tried out for junior varsity basketball, but the coach had only twelve uniforms. Three people had to go. It was evident who two of them were—that was a no-brainer from the start. Billy, however, was in a battle for the final spot—a two-horse race with Sean Paisemore.

Billy had lost sleep the night before—he knew what the cards were, and he knew it was going to come down to the final practice. He went over the practice drills in his mind and tried to be positive; he pictured himself hitting the open man, drilling the open jumper, creating space for his teammates, the whole picture.

Late in the final practice, things were still close. Billy hadn't been doing anything great, but neither had Sean. With seconds to go in the scrimmage, and with the score tied, Billy dribbled up, planning on cutting off a screen and firing it to his center. The play started perfectly—in fact, he could still see it all unfold even years later: the center breaking from his man, the perfectly set screen, Billy running his opponent into the screen, and moving off to make the pass.

And it all went perfectly—until Billy dribbled the ball off of his foot and out of bounds. The other team got the ball, scored just inside the buzzer, and Billy's team was beaten. He was cut, by the way; he was the last man out.

That's a horrible story!

Not true; it's a beautiful story. Billy went on to switch to soccer and became an All-Area player by his junior year. Things *do* work out for the best, you know. You just have to stay positive, forgive yourself, and keep moving forward.

Where'd that story come from?

You see, that's my point. Every smell, every piece of litter, every slamming locker, every voice, every bell—they all brought up story after story after story. Just the smell of ammonia brought me overtime wins and losses, tryouts, boys and girls flirting with each other, scoring error screw-ups, buzzer baskets, heroes and goats, arguments between coaches and officials—the list is almost literally endless. And sit tight, I hadn't even left the broom closet yet—hadn't even straightened out my collared shirt and entrenched the hat firmly over my eyebrows. I wasn't even in the hallways yet! I even thought of you a couple of times!

Really? I'm impressed! What happened?

A guy asked a girl to the Winterfest Dance and she said no. That was the first time. The second time was when a boy left Latin class after making a forty-eight on his quiz. Oh, those two tales so reminded me of your attempts at growing up. But let me continue.

Well, I'm not going to interrupt God! You're like a little kid at Christmas.

What, you don't think God gets excited? I'm you humans' biggest cheerleader—just give me a set of pom-poms and a skirt, and I'll yell for you endlessly. And I mean that almost literally.

It's just fun to picture, that's all. Sorry to interrupt; I'll shut up now.

To give my day another two-word description, it would be "awesome squared." Again, I felt everything. There was all that energy and every emotion I've ever invented flying across and around, all begging for attention. The grid was so full it was almost solid, if that makes any sense. And trust me, I can't say it better than that so you might understand. The basic thrust was "notice me, see me, listen to me" as I stood in sophomore hall. I felt the rebels who just wanted to make a C and get high school life over with, I felt the social butterflies who gadded about from locker to locker collecting the "dirt," I felt the jocks who wore their accomplishments like a prize or an Olympic medal, and I felt the misfits who just wanted to be accepted. I felt it all, and everything in between. I'll repeat—it was sensory overload, and it was wonderfully irreverent.

Okay, tell me more.

I was in the hallway sweeping. My head was down, and I was just fascinated by what had accumulated on the floors of the school.

So are most parents, but go ahead.

Let me give you an example. Crumpled up by one of the lockers was a test score—it was a Spanish quiz graded eighty-nine; Leigh Collins was the student. I picked it up and felt everything—the whole story. Leigh was very disappointed by that grade—she's an A student trying to get into the Ivy League—she had actually shed a tear over the eighty-nine even though it was only a quiz and will count as a very small portion of her final score. She had meant to study more—she really had—but she found herself the night before getting interested in a *CSI Miami* episode and fell asleep on her couch. When driving to school the next day, she told herself that it was no big deal and that she'd simply study during first period and ace the test—no problem. However, a fire alarm sounded during first period. She had to leave the building with all the other students, and that "threw her off her game." Once back inside, she found herself gossiping about the upcoming weekend, hence the "bad" grade of eighty-nine on the quiz. In fact, that's the reason the test was on the floor in the first place—she angrily threw it there after she got it back after class. She stepped on it on purpose as she walked away and headed to American Lit; she carried it with her mentally for a couple of hours. I felt all this just from picking it up off the floor—I felt her frustration, her anger—mostly at herself—and her dreams of heading up east for college. Again, I cheer for her—believe it or not I *am* in you peoples' corners. I *do* want you to succeed; I *do* want you to "get it." I'm excited for you; I'm excited being a part of you. Now dang it, *use* me. Listen to me. Hear me. Take me with you—and not just over weekends when you play tennis and write stories and flirt with cocktail waitresses. You people, as much as I love you, can and do frustrate me to tears—a lot of the time.

I'm actually feeling your frustration.

Good, use it wisely! Now let me proceed—I could talk all day about my time in the sophomore hallway at your school. Thanks, by the way—for risking your job in sneaking me in. One time I thought I was actually going to get caught. I had to hide briefly in Lab 4 when a real janitor came by. Thought I was screwed for sure. Boy, don't get me started on how I briefly felt while *inside* a classroom; I'm just glad I wasn't seen.

Why didn't you disappear inside a wall or something or vanish into thin air? I mean, you are God.

I am a God who is powerless and not allowed in your schools—you keep forgetting that! Now, let me tell you about the bracelet I found—a seemingly innocent bracelet lying broken on the floor in front of locker number 2089. It was snapped in two and dirty; it had been trodden upon. Its appearance was so miniscule that not one kid noticed it between first and second period. All simply went about with their energies and their hidden agendas, their ideas and plans. They exchanged books, gossiped, slammed lockers, and carried forward—just doing the "cosmic dance," as I like to call it. The bracelet belonged to Angie Peterson—Thomas Clairmont gave it to her. Thomas, for the record, is forever madly in love with Angie—hook, line, and sinker. He fantasizes about her daily, not to mention nightly; he follows her in his thoughts; and he often visualizes the two walking hand-in-hand to class.

Unfortunately, the love isn't reciprocated. Angie finds him "mildly amusing" but views him more as a pest. She made it very clear to him that the two are just friends and nothing more. Still, Thomas held to that "friends" comment and amplified it with vision after vision after vision.

To go on, Angie was taking off her sweater in the hallway the other day after coming in for school. While lifting it off her arms, she yanked the bracelet and it snapped. She never even saw it hit the floor and, quite frankly, never even missed it. She simply resumed her agenda for the day in her head, went to class, and all that.

Poor Thomas, though! The second he saw her *not* wearing that bracelet, he went into a mental tailspin. He still hasn't gotten over it, and it happened a week ago. He bombed a Government test because of it—his concentration was shot.

Don't you have any stories with happy endings?

Don't you see—they *all* have happy endings! Haven't you heard the saying, "If it doesn't end well, then it's not really the end"? The two would've been miserable; it would've been like you and Gail Thompson all over again. Thomas will get over it and will become a better man because of it. Angie will go about her life—the two's lives will never intersect again after high school—and both will live out their talents—I hope so anyway. Things happen for your own good—please know that! Write that down! They might not *seem* so good once they happen, but stay positive. *Trust* that I know what I'm doing. I'll say that again—*trust* that I know what I'm doing. Quit shaking your fists at me and cussing me! Use me for your own good. I'm here, and I'm your biggest fan—I'm all of you peoples' biggest fan.

I'm glad you had such a good time today.

I'm more than grateful for my time today. I didn't want to be anywhere else in the world other than where I was—ironically, where I'm not allowed. I considered myself the unofficial "director of morale," and I blended in perfectly. In fact, you once looked right through me—never thought twice; just kept on worrying about going over your tennis budget. By the way, you might want to work on that. Anyway, I had the Morgan Freeman thing going—picture him with an engineer's cap pulled down over his eyes. Kids walked right past me, to and fro, all full of pep and vinegar. Some spoke, most didn't; all were busy little bees in their own little lives.

I wanted to get into a conversation with them all—every one of them. Like I said, I was your dog, Jasper—just give me a sniff and I'll tell you a tale. A couple of times I had to go back inside the broom closet—doubled over again in what I can only describe as an excellent pain.

Tell me more. I'd much rather hear about your day than you about mine.

Don't you have somewhere to be?

What do you mean? I love your stories.

I hate to interrupt, but the bell just rang. You're late for your own class!

God Gets Left Behind

Where have you been?

I've been gone since Wednesday; I was in Jekyll Island at a Georgia tennis coaches' workshop. It was awesome!

Well, did you take me with you?

Um …

Think twice before answering; you don't want to lie to God! Now, did you even consider me while you were away?

Well, I didn't want to interrupt.

So you went to the beach for three days, and the last you saw me I was sweeping the sophomore hallways of your school!

I thought you loved it!

I did; I was being sarcastic. But that's not the point. Did you take me with you? Or did you at least bring me a T-shirt?

Well, yes, I got a Jekyll Island Coaches' Workshop shirt.

No, I wanted one with "Hard Rock Cafe" written on it.

God likes Hard Rock Cafe T-shirts?

Yes, I collect them. I've got London, Cancun, San Francisco, and Atlanta. Don't they have one in Jekyll Island? I've also got a shirt that reads, "I'm not 50 years old; I'm 18 with 32 years experience!"

I like that! Still, you should know—being God and all—that they do not have a Hard Rock Cafe in Jekyll Island.

Yes but you're missing my point.

Which is?

You had a perfectly good weekend last weekend with me. You took me with you, I sent you signs, you received them. I sent you Deepak on Facebook, I sent you a song or two on the radio—Bananarama not included. I sent you a message from your girls' golf coach. I followed you to the tennis courts. You had a wonderful, clean match. You took me with you when you wrote up your tennis match and even into the shower. And then what do you do? You go flitting around in Jekyll and don't even buy me a T-shirt! Now don't you see why I get so frustrated with you humans? We have a perfectly good thing going, and then you just forget! And get this, even when you think things aren't going smoothly, they really are in the long run. I'm trying to take care of you people, and what do you do? You forget! Again!

Well, what can I tell you. You're right!

Of course I'm right! Did you forget whom you are talking to? Now, tell me about your weekend; spare me nothing.

I drove that wonderful interstate known as I-16—163 miles of nothing but cement and pine trees and the uneven grooves of that horrible road. No exits, no restaurants, just road and the hum of my car. And cops sitting all over the place—saw two even before I hit Dublin. You're right; I could've used you there; you could've been my radar detector. Kidding, of course. I got there around four thirty and immediately met Skip, his wife, and a couple of tennis friends for drinks in the bar.

Don't you have a funny story about the cops on I-16?

Yes, but I don't think my readers wants to hear about me with a gun to my back on the side of the road and my having an unplanned bowel movement on the spot. Sorry to be so crude with God, but that's about the size of it.

And I seem to remember you wrote up the incident and showed it to your boss, who loved it, and that's why you decided to become a writer in the first place. In fact, that was about the only time you talked to me that year—the afternoon you had a handgun at your back. You never thanked me for getting you out of that mess, by the way.

Thanks from the bottom of my heart. Can we continue?

Okay, to continue … you got smashed before dinner?

I wasn't going to put it that way, but I did have three glasses of red wine and was feeling pretty good. Somehow I just couldn't picture you having a good time down there.

Lame excuse, but go ahead.

We then went to dinner across the grounds on the pier, and a less-than-enthusiastic waitress waited on us.

Hey, lay off of her! She's struggling to make ends meet, she's going through a rough patch, and she doesn't particularly like her job. I hope you people weren't rude to her.

I wasn't.

Good! There are two things every human on your planet should have to do before they move on—wait tables and officiate some type of sporting contest in front of a big crowd.

I'm happy to say I've done both.

And I'm quick to say you weren't very happy in either case, but go ahead.

Thursday there was an indoor seminar before we went to the courts.

Did you listen?

I tried my best.

And how did you do? You really should check on your ADD. You've got the attention span of a splattering gnat on a windshield. Sorry to keep interrupting.

We hit the courts after that, and it rocked! It was sunny and around fifty-five degrees, and we played for about two hours.

How'd you hit them?

Horrible, but who cares?

Nobody but you and perhaps your mixed doubles partners, but go ahead. Continue with your details of this trip you never once thought of me on.

We knocked off around five thirty and then all met out for dinner at Spanky's around seven. See, I just can't imagine taking God to a place called Spanky's. Can't imagine sitting around shooting the … I mean, talking to God over a Blue Moon beer or a Merlot. Somehow this just doesn't fit!

And somehow this is where you all mess up! You think you can only talk to me on Sundays in church. I would've loved to go to Spanky's, by the way. I would've worn my janitor's cap and my jeans! Their shrimp rocks, though their fries are sometimes a bit overcooked. Still, you could have introduced me as your doubles partner or your agent. Don't get me wrong; I wouldn't have shared a drink with you, but still. And speaking of which, might I introduce you to this drink called water? I hear good things about it, and it's free! No hangovers, no headaches, it costs you nothing, and it's actually healthy. Seriously, try it sometime! Slip it into your diet somewhere between your Chick-fil-A lemonade and your Merlot. It might do you some good. Now go ahead, tell me more of what I missed.

Well, I felt isolated the whole time, which was good. If you have Sprint as your cell carrier, you might as well not have a phone. I mean, I love Jekyll, and I like Sprint, but the cell service is a bit lax—no towers on the island, I was told.

Perhaps that was my sign—you felt isolated. No cell phones, you left your laptop computer at home, you had no electronic method of communication whatsoever. You forgot me, so you felt isolated. Run that through your ADD brain for a second.

Point taken. Anyway, Friday morning we had another morning lecture—which, by the way, I actually participated in. Then we hit the courts, and that was it!

Then you spent Friday at your friend Pride's, and you woke up early Saturday morning and made the five-hour drive in less than five hours. See? Even after your past episode on I-16, you still drove too fast! Did I not make my point with the cop and the handgun?

Oops! Then I drove home to what was a beautiful "spring feverish" weekend in Atlanta. It got up to almost seventy degrees Saturday and Sunday.

Well, did you get out and play, or did you screw around in your house the whole time?

I got out! I ran at the river, went to my team's mixed match Sunday, and spent as much time outside as I possibly could! Don't worry; I'm not going to bore you with another one of my tennis stories. Still, it's too bad it's supposed to get cold again. I'm over it!

Let's move on. Might I suggest you use me while I'm here? What do you want to discuss, talk about, solve, get rid of, or answer? How may I serve? You seem distracted anyway; spill it! You've got God right here.

What, another touchdown?

No, a man in Iowa wants to know if he should run for president or not. I simply must help him.

You're going to encourage him, right?

Yes, I'm going to encourage him not to; he'd be horrible! I'll be right back!

God, Divorce, and a Case of Depression

Okay, God, I've got an assignment for you. The year is 2006. My wife just gave me the boot, I'm lonely, I'm depressed, and I just lost the love of my life—my dog Jasper. I challenge you to make this funny. Ready ... set ... go!

Wow! If I didn't know better, I'd say this was a healthy attitude on your part.

Really?

Yes, really! You want to recall what was the absolute worst part of your life and be able to laugh about it. Good for you! Most people carry the worst parts to their graves, and that's often the reason they get to their graves in the first place! You actually want to laugh about it. Bravo! Bravo! Bravo!

I'm actually getting a compliment from God! I should stop right now and end this manuscript—quit while I'm ahead. Maybe there is hope for me after all!

Don't get carried away.

You're right, but today is my five-year divorce-aversary!

Obviously this is something we need to discuss. So many people these days are getting divorced that we might as well.

It was February, and it was a Tuesday—don't know why I remember that. I'd just gotten up in our wonderful South Florida home to go get some coffee from—of course—Dunkin' Donuts. I walked down the stairs, mattress marks still on my face, and politely asked my wife of about fifteen more minutes if she wanted me to pick her up some coffee as well. She liked hers black, and she always got mad because they'd put cream in it. Always!

And what did she say?

She said the words you *never*—and I mean *never*—want to hear when you're in a relationship. She said, "Sit down; we need to talk." Whenever you hear those six words, run—don't walk—out of the room, because the game as you know it is now over. Complete. Game, set, match.

And you didn't run? You even had on your Nike running shoes! What's with you; why didn't you take off?

Cute. She proceeded to tell me how she wasn't happy and how things were better when we were married and I was looking after the house in Atlanta while she was going to school in Charleston (another story). And how we probably needed to see a counselor, though I could tell that ship had already sailed. And how I needed to wipe my nose because something was dribbling out of it. And she complimented me on my latest zit.

Actually, you're lying there at the end, but how did you respond?

What could I say? I could tell by her tone that she had already checked out and that lately we had been nothing more than compatible roommates who shared pets. My mind was already ticking—who would get Jasper? She could have that darn bird and the sugar glider and the two rats and the two cats. Just give me Jasper or give me death! That dog was a pain in the butt, but I freaking *loved* him. I still do. In fact, I eventually got over my wife, but I *never* got over Jasper. Anyway, speaking of getting over my wife, today is the day I'm officially supposed to be over her.

Why do you say that?

Because they—whoever "they" are—say that it takes half the time you were in a relationship to get over it. We were together ten years, and today is our fifth divorce-aversary, so as of 12:01 a.m., I'm officially supposed to be "over her."

Are you? And you're saying you humans have a formula for how long it's supposed to take different souls to get over somebody?

Sure, though I must admit I heard a lot of advice after my divorce. You'd never believe how many "experts" come out of the woodwork, both before you get married and after you get divorced. I've never heard so much unsolicited advice in my life. And I didn't ask a one of them! I can't tell you how many times people told me to "get back on the horse."

What did you tell them?

I told them it was pretty darned hard to get back on the proverbial horse when you're still in midair from falling!

Cute, but let's continue; I take it you never made it to coffee that day?

Oh, I made it—I always get my coffee. I just didn't have to bring back another cup because she wasn't there when I got back, which was *very* sad. In fact, just last night I dreamed we'd gotten back together and I woke up very happy. Why is it that even though you know it's for the best for both of you, it still gets to you sometimes?

I know this must be bugging you, because even you're having a hard time being funny about this. Why is that? This is the time when you need to be laughing the most!

Once again, I missed the signs, though I will say this: My doctor gave me a test—scoring range was zero through forty. If you scored a ten or higher, you were depressed. I scored a twenty-two! A twenty-two! Now, that wasn't "put a gun in my mouth" depressed, but I can assure you I had no interest in anything. And like I said earlier, depression is nothing more than a mental and physical paralysis. *Nothing* sounded good, nothing mattered, and I couldn't have cared less about anything or anybody. Rude, maybe, but there it is. My days were spent lying in bed, staring at walls. I beat myself up pretty badly. I don't think I laughed for a month, and of course, that was once again at Jasper when he peed all over himself and had that ignorant look on his face. Classic!

I remember, but before this gets too heavy, tell us your quick story of why your relationship failed when you were a junior in college. That's sad, but quite funny.

Well, my girlfriend approached me at the tennis courts. She told me this: "After I graduate, I'm going to go to Georgia to get my master's, I'm going to counsel for two years after that, and then I'm going to teach. What are you going to do?"

And your answer?

After putting down my tennis racket, I said, "Well, it's Thursday. I'll probably go to the pub around ten thirty."

And she didn't want to stick around with you after that? Boy, I'm shocked!

There you go with your sarcasm again. It wasn't funny at the time, but boy did my college buddies—male and female—give me a hard time about that one. In fact, I'm still asked to this very day—thirty-one years later—to tell that story.

Like I said—you always have been good for a few laughs. And I must admit, you tell the story quite well!

Thanks, I think, but let's continue.

Yes, you were discussing your ex-wife and your dog and how you hated that "damn bird." You also seemed to be worried because you incorrectly thought that you were struggling alone and your ex just waltzed into another relationship immediately thereafter.

I was wrong?

Yes. Haven't you heard the saying, "The woman gets depressed about a year or more before the divorce; the guys do the suffering a year or more after"?

Where'd you hear that?

I either read it or I made it up.

I guess you'd given up on trying to send me signs at this point—after the Bee Gees and "Tragedy" and all that.

You're right; I sent them to her instead.

Really?

Yes, and she picks up on things better than you.

What were her signs?

On her five-mile drive to work, she heard the song "Hit the Road Jack" about three times. Man, was that sign sent and delivered! She couldn't wait to get her size-six foot up your rear and have you out that door!

A disgusting visual!

Yes, kind of like your marriage!

Touché! I guess I can laugh about this time because nothing was working!

Not true, your poor Honda Civic worked just fine! It got you from North Palm to Madison, Georgia, back to North Palm, up to Lancaster, Pennsylvania, back down to North Palm, and eventually to Atlanta. Some of Jackson Browne's lyrics applied to you at this point: "No matter how fast I run, I can never seem to get away from me."

Awesome! Love Jackson Browne! Saw him in concert once; he played in Tampa with Tom Petty! Great show!

Still, your finally getting settled back in Georgia reminded me of a song.

What, another Jackson Browne classic—"Running on Empty"?

No, the Charlie Daniels Band—"The Devil Went Down to Georgia"!

I am *so* glad you brought that song up! I don't want to get tossed in the burning fires of hell for this, but the devil's fiddle is *so* much better than Johnny's in that song. It's not even close! I never did understand that song. How could they think Johnny won? I'm not a fan of the devil or anything—I don't want to sign up for the wrong team, but still—there was major injustice done in that song!

Do you really want to talk about that song? Now continue with your poor-me story—your "public" is waiting!

I got back from coffee that day, and the silence practically killed me. I remember this: I sat on the stairwell—no job to speak of, no wife, no real desire to be living away from home in Georgia, no real anything. There I sat, head in hands, a full-fledged failure in *every* sense of the word. Without a pot to pee in and with no end in sight, I remember smiling because of Jasper.

What did he do? Did he pee again?

No, he trotted up those stairs and sat right beside me. It was as if he were saying, "I'm still with you, master. You hang in there. Wherever you go, I go." This reminds me, may I ask a favor of you, God, though I know I don't deserve it?

You all deserve it; now go ahead.

When I die and cruise into the great beyond, if there is any truth to crossing the pearly gates, I want my daddy to be standing there with Jasper on a leash. Now don't get me wrong, I still want to see the grandparents, the aunts, the uncles, etc., but I want to be met by my dad and my dog. And I don't want Jasper to be cured of his problem—I want to see him hike up that leg at least one more time—the look on his face is priceless!

Of all your loved ones and of all your memories, you want to see your dog hike up his leg? You should have quit earlier at "Bravo! Bravo!"

Sorry, I didn't mean to question God. But about this, where were the signs? Where were my Deepak quotes or my chance encounters? Where was the movie or the commercial or something to spark the something to let me know or give me a warning? There I was, all cold, wet, and lonely down in South Florida, and without my Bee Gees eight-track tapes!

Actually, one of the Bee Gees died in Miami while you were down there.

That's a pretty harsh sign, don't you think?

I'm just saying. Still, you were working part-time at Barnes & Noble for seven bucks an hour, and you were covering polo and equestrian, for my sake. What in the world do you know about polo and equestrian?

I know what a horse looks like, and I know that the horse and the rider are supposed to be facing the same way.

Very cute. Now continue. Nothing was working, and you weren't happy. Worse yet, a Bee Gee had died and you were off getting your coffee without anyone to share it with. Your credit cards had hernias from keeping you afloat, *Big Bang Theory* and *Two and a Half Men* hadn't been invented yet, and you were sick of tennis, so watching any of the four majors just didn't do it for you. Is that about right?

Don't forget about my accident on I-95—the night where a van full of punks rammed me from behind doing eighty. I could've been killed!

You're welcome, by the way!

I remember chasing that van down a side street.

And?

And after a couple of miles I started thinking, *What am I going to do if I actually catch these people and they actually stop?* It's not like in the movies, where they all attack one at a time. Still, with lightning reflexes, I Bruce Lee one, kung fu another, use my MacGyver-like smarts to slay another, and then book the other like Jack Lord in the old *Hawaii Five-O* episodes. Seriously, what was I going to do?

Keeping in mind that your fighting record is 0–28, I'd say you made the right choice! You really should be laughing about all this. Besides, tell both of your readers how things are going for you now.

They are going unbelievably well. Once this "devil" got back to Georgia, everything started working. The person who coached the same sports as I did left the school, leaving both jobs open for me. The school made changes in the Communications/Public Relations Department, leaving doors open for me. I found a condo for less than half of what I planned on paying for it, and it was located only two miles from the school. I was back with my old friends, I started playing tennis again, and the prices at Dunkin' Donuts were even better than they were in North Palm. And to top it off, I had the Hub Channel on cable, where I could watch *Doogie Howser* and *Wonder Years* episodes—not to mention *Happy Days*—for hours on end. I mean, how could life be any better? Though I could have done without *Laverne and Shirley.*

Lay off Laverne and Shirley! And quit watching so much television! Get a life, and this is coming straight from God! Now, moving on, don't you see? Don't you remember what I made you stress earlier? When you're in the right place, doing the things you are supposed to be doing, you will *always* get the breaks. Have you forgotten this already? Now, in your head, compare life when you got back home to life in South Florida. Don't you see the difference? Did I have to send another Bee Gees song, or wasn't it quite obvious? But let's move ahead. You, being as stubborn as you are, still had questions, I believe, as late as August of last summer. Please continue.

Okay, my friend Phil took a two-year job in Beirut, Lebanon. He's now the assistant middle school principal at the American School in Beirut. I drove him to the airport on Monday, August 16—don't ask me why I remember that date, but I do.

Why do you remember that date—it's completely irrelevant! What was going through your head after he boarded—I mean besides the nightly TV schedule you were going to speed home to?

I was questioning myself again—wondering why I didn't have the guts to go overseas and why I was such a homebody and why I couldn't be doing something cool like that.

You are a hardheaded soul, but continue please.

I remember walking to my car at the airport, dreading the drive home. I mean, it was five o'clock and I was faced with the task of driving straight through downtown Atlanta or getting on I-285—neither sounding better than the other during rush hour.

And?

And I drove straight through town, got on I-285 east, got off at Roswell Road, and had absolutely *zero* traffic! I only had to slow down once—just before getting onto 285. Besides that it was one of the smoother Atlanta rides during traffic I remember.

And you think this was a coincidence? Or maybe it was me telling you that the reason for the "no traffic thing" was that you, too, were going *exactly* where you were supposed to be going, when you were supposed to be going there. Now, I'm not saying you'll never hit traffic in Atlanta—give me a break; that's too big a task even for God to handle. And I promise MARTA is getting better—a lot better. But think of it this way: At the exact time you were questioning where you

were supposed to be—why you were questioning after all of the above signs I'll never know—you drove through town with no traffic. You got from the airport to your condo in less than thirty minutes. That's unheard of for a "normal" Monday-through-Friday drive in Atlanta. It just doesn't happen—but it did!

I think I actually got that sign. If I remember right, I smiled and pointed my finger up in the air at you when I parked at home.

You needn't do that—I'm busy enough with athletes. Still, you want to laugh? How's this since we're talking about former spouses: I ran into my ex the other day. Then I put it in reverse and ran into her again! How's that?

That's horrible!

Sorry, I got that off of Facebook. I'm—hold it—someone just scored a hockey goal in Toronto. I'll be right back.

Okay, sorry about that; that one always calls my name. Why is it that you humans always feel so alone during the times you need me most? Remember last weekend, when you took me with you? Did you feel alone? Did you feel left out? Did you feel depressed? No, I kept you busy—even your ADD head was pretty focused on what was going on—on what matters, anyway. You read my signs, you went with them, you exercised, and you didn't even drink as much as you normally do. Consider this a major breakthrough!

Then I promptly went off to Jekyll Island and forgot all about you.

Something I've already forgiven you for, yet you won't accept it. Why is that? I'm God, and I've forgotten; who the heck are you to remember? Do I need to put it that way? Do I need to say it again? Do you need to write it on your bathroom mirror?

Hmm, that's a great way of putting it. How'd you come up with that? I mean … never mind. Still, I have a question: why is it that the *only* thing that is sure in life is that when you're trying to get over someone, you will *always* bump into them? And I do mean, *always*—no exceptions, *ever*! I walked out of a store in the mall the next day, and my ex and I literally almost bumped into each other headfirst!

I thought that was hilarious! If you had walked out of that smoothie place literally a second sooner, you two would have collided—face-to-face. Abbott and Costello or the Three Stooges couldn't have pulled it off any better.

As for your lesson, you were to move forward in peace but to remember the lessons of the past. I literally almost slammed you to into each other as a reminder that the marriage is over; there was no doubt in either of your heads. You were to bump into each other on purpose whereas not to forget some things. She was with her new man; you were about to move north, and you were wondering why you didn't order the Immune Builder instead of the Angel Food. Both of you were going to forget some things that needn't be forgotten. Yes, it was a bit perverse—and yes, if you could've seen the looks on the two of your faces, you might've laughed. Still, you both got through it, and you're better off because of it. Remember Nietzsche: "What does not kill us only makes us stronger."

I contend that it almost killed me.

Nope, don't forget: if I can lead you to it, I can lead you through it. I cut it close—I took you to the desert—but you were brought back, and you're better and stronger because of it—as is she. Now your job is to remember and forget at the same time. Got it?

For now … until I forget again.

I'll remind you; trust me on that one. Now, move on! You've read the saying: "If you're heading in the right direction, just keep going." Get out of your comfort zone! Speaking of which, share with us your quote about comfort zones.

Sure, my saying is, "Comfort zones are for people who don't have the guts to keep growing." I actually thought of that all by myself. Still, I could never figure out if I should end it with "growing" or "going," but I guess the meaning is the same.

The meaning is the same, and I gave you those words while you were out drinking at Taco Mac with your Oglethorpe coaching buddies. (Another story; we probably won't have time for them here). You said those well-polished words—one of your fellow coaches even wrote it down, posted it on her door, and gave you full credit. She even spelled your name right.

Coming up with sayings is the easy part—it's incorporating them into the daily grind that's not always so easy.

That's because you don't trust me!

Okay, I'll work on that. But let's sum things up here: it's been five years—where's my new woman? Seriously?

Okay, seriously, you just got back from Jekyll Island. Where's my T-shirt?

More Solutions from the Grand Master

I have a good question—maybe it's personal, and maybe it pertains to a lot of people. Why is my mind a total human cesspool? On some days, it's like there are a bunch of rabid zombie ferrets running through my skull, each thought vying for my attention, each one crankier than the one before. By lunch I'm a mess and nothing really bad has happened! What's up with that? Why do warmongers, evil spirits, and the good old-fashioned devil himself invade my mind? I mean, what did I do to deserve this?

Did you actually just say rabid zombie ferrets?

I did, and on purpose even!

Okay, enlighten me. Don't just complain—remember, I hate complaining—give me a specific example or two. Are you having a tough day today?

I am! And for no real reason! Okay, let's take this morning: First I had a bad dream—and no, it wasn't about my ex-wife, may she live long and prosper and enough about that. However, Dunkin' Donuts (gasp) was out of French Vanilla—a horrible crime if there ever was one. It was raining outside with an outside chance of sleet later on, thus raining out tennis—again. One of my substitute teachers broke her leg and just called, so I had to get on the phone and find her a replacement. So while my mind is shifting into incredibly low gear, I just realize I've ordered the wrong sizes in long-sleeved T-shirts for my tennis team. You're a T-shirt man; surely you see the crime in that? Seriously, what would you do if one of your Hard Rock Cafe shirts were the wrong size?

This would be a modern-day tragedy if there ever was one, but go ahead.

I get to school and park, and upon getting out of my car, I step into this huge crater of a mud puddle, getting crap all over my unironed khaki pants. On top of all this, I fell asleep last night and did *not* get to watch reruns of *The Wonder Years* on the Hub Channel—another heinous crime. So now the first bell hasn't even rung and I'm cruising into "things that irritate Dunn today." The list is endless, and it's getting bigger: no Super Bowl party to go to, a teacher forgot to leave her rolls for the substitute, the boss just walked by without speaking (Is he mad? Did I do something wrong?), I still haven't heard about my potential promotion, my accountant hasn't called regarding my taxes, and I'm running out of patience.

You see! Nothing major has happened yet, and I'm kicked into underdrive—I'm trying to take control of my mind, but the rabid zombie ferrets are kicking 152 percent of my butt! And it's getting worse!

I hate to interrupt when you're on such a roll, but may I?

Of course. You're God; you can pretty much do whatever you want. You don't have a boss waving a promotion carrot under your nose.

You poor thing, and yes that was sarcasm at its finest and to the nth degree. Now allow me to interject your bickering with a simple statement. The solution is quite literally as plain as the nose on your face. And I'm not playing tricks with you; I couldn't mean it more simply.

Please explain. The nose on my face is filled to the brim. I think I'm catching cold. Oh yeah, that's something I forgot to mention, though—of course—I'm not complaining! LOL.

Did you just use a texting term when talking to God? Hmm, texting God—perhaps we'll get into that later, or maybe we won't. Anyway, don't you remember as a kid when you got mad and your mother told you to take deep breaths? Or maybe she told you to count to ten? She probably did both.

Yes, but taking deep breaths and counting to ten at the same time was a bit difficult for me.

Cute, but there it is—your answer lies in your breath. And you can forget counting if you want to. It's the simple act of breathing. When you get stressed, the breath becomes shallow, quicker. The answer is to slow down your breathing. The next time all of these "tragedies" occur, simply stop what you are doing and take at least three slow, deep breaths, concentrating ONLY on the art of breathing. Get to at least three and force yourself to slow down. Do this as often as possible during your cesspool-filled day and you will be amazed. Who knows—it might even help you "stop the bleeding," so to speak. You can kill off each zombie ferret one at a time. It works better than Raid on roaches. (More on that later).

It will simply stop your mind from going to where it's going—will put the brakes on—and you can regroup and refocus, and who knows, *The Wonder Years* might be on again tonight! What a problem solver!

It can't be that simple.

Why not—because it doesn't cost anything? Because it doesn't take a lot of time? Because it's not complicated? Because even a child can understand it? Because you're feeling like an idiot because it is so

easy? Pick one, but take my advice. We even spoke earlier in this book about using your shower time to internalize and focus—to get your day planned and off on the right foot. I use the shower because you Americans are always "too busy" for me. Some of you even run off to Jekyll and forget about me. Ironic as it is, the times you need me most are the times I'm most forgotten. Still, it's an ongoing issue and a game I will win eventually. You people just take time, that's all.

Do you think it would be humanly possible for me to go one complete day—just one—with nothing but gratitude and thanks and happiness and peace of mind and joy?

With your mind, not a chance!

Good Lord!

Yes, I am a good Lord, but that's not the point. And I was kidding; the question is, do you think you can?

Unfortunately, I don't think I can do it.

Then there's your answer.

Well, how do you know you can if you know you can't?

Humor yourself. Tell yourself you can. Or break the day down into segments. Don't take a full day—that might appear too much. Take an hour, take thirty minutes, take five minutes, and then try to add to that each day. Come on; you're a coach—you don't have people running the full marathon on the first day, do you? You don't have people hitting topspin lobs in their first lesson, do you?

That would be dumb.

Then don't be dumb with yourself!

You know, you actually make pretty good sense.

Ahem.

Just kidding.

Okay, coach, challenge yourself—and report back to me with it. Pick a time segment, go through with it, and tell me all about it. I want to hear every detail in that slimy mind of yours—where it goes, where it stops, what prevents it from being happy, what makes you leave me to go watch mindless sitcoms—the whole nine yards.

Do I have to be completely honest?

No! You can keep lying to yourself and get completely nowhere during this lifetime. You'd be surprised at how many people do just that. Yes, be completely honest—tell me where your mind goes, and I'll try to help you stay on track.

You'd do that for me?

What? Do you think I'm mean? Do you not think I'm here to help? I'd be afraid to ask you what you think my role is in all this. Write these words down; share them with everyone in this manuscript—I *am on your side*! Did you get that?

Okay, okay, I've got it. Now, if you don't mind, tidy up the junior hallway, and I'll come slip you a note after study hall. I've got a free period after my second-to-last history class. The kids are working on a project, so I'll use that period as my guinea pig. Wish me luck, would you?

I am always wishing you luck! Now get back to work!

(Later that day, I almost forgot to keep my appointment with God. It seems there was a complaint that sophomore hallway was *much* cleaner than the others, so the powers that be were either looking to fire the janitors in the other hallways or promote the one on sophomore hall—whichever came first. Still, something did happen that brought me back to speaking to the Great One.)

You know, you really crack me up. You really do have a sense of humor.

Why, whatever are you talking about?

Don't play dumb with me; I'll never buy it when God tries to play dumb.

Are you telling me you have a report on your experiment? Are you telling me I can't be dumb when I want to? You can, but I can't? That's hardly fair.

Don't get me started on fairness! But let's not digress! I was walking down the hall on an hour break between classes. Frankly, I was bored. It was after lunch, so I was tired, my mind was as fresh as a sewer-ridden gutter, and I just wanted a couch to sit down on. Already I'd forgotten my plan to have my happy day, so I just walked into a coworker's office and plopped onto her couch. "You can stay if you want, but I've got a class coming in," she said. "We're just going to be doing some relaxing stuff and some reading."

So I stayed in there. I'm reading this book called *What to Say When You Talk to Yourself*, which is pretty interesting, so I opened it up while the class came in. Lo and behold, the teacher—after everyone had gathered around—started talking about how this is the time of day when our minds go negative, this is the time of day when we get tired, blah, blah, blah. It was exactly what I was thinking and feeling.

And?

And she had the class go through a meditation. She had us focus on our breath, in and out. She had us lift up our arms in yogalike fashion. She had us close our eyes. Everything she was doing was in line with what you and I talked about earlier, but I had already chosen to forget. Like I said, you crack me up!

Ask and you shall receive—haven't you ever heard that before?

About a zillion times, but I've never really listened to it—or believed it.

Your attention—we've already discussed that—had already gone to tennis practice, to your IRS refund, to spring training baseball, and the lot. You'd already shucked your idea of watching your thoughts, even though we had just had the conversation not two hours earlier. Love your memory, by the way—just love it! This time, however, I wasn't going to let you get off so easily. Hence, your "random" decision to sit in your friend's office. Hence, her lecture on meditation and deep breathing. Hence, your laughing at me for the way I reminded you. See, I do have a way of my own.

It was terribly embarrassing, though; you know that, don't you?

How so?

When she started talking about controlling your breath and thus controlling your thoughts, I started laughing out loud. The whole class— including the teacher—stared at me, thinking I was being rude or not believing her. I thought I was going to get thrown out of class even though my days of getting thrown out of class—I hope—are long gone. I had to apologize to her later and tell her what had happened.

And she was very supportive.

You know that she was. She even told me to tell you to pretend that she was sitting in the back of the end zone, bowing to you—she needs a little help herself. Pretend she just broke through for a twenty-three-yard scoring touchdown. There she is on one knee, her head tilted up, calling your name. She laughed, but I think she was serious.

She was. Message received. Send her a message, though, will you? Tell her it's not necessary to take her helmet off. I can hear her just fine!

Thoughts, Cameras, Action!

This is fun; hit me with some more wisdom. I need all the help I can get. What else should I carry with me as I go to and fro from work each day?

Well, go to your meetings for a change. Your colleagues might be glad to see you. Seriously, reintroduce yourself. Shake a hand or two.

No, seriously.

Okay, I think everyone should live their lives as if television cameras were trained on them.

Ouch! Terribly embarrassing!

You used to do it as a kid, remember? You pretended all your classmates were watching you outside of school.

And I repeat: Terribly embarrassing! I'm picturing this as I write: a camera hanging out in the places of ill repute I've been known to hang out at—on a Friday or Saturday night even.

You'd do well to do my assignment, or take me in there with you in your mind. It worked the other weekend, didn't it?

Yes, but jogging and tennis are pretty innocent activities, though Saturday night was a bit shady. I'm previewing my weekend in my head and picturing a TV camera in front of me. Granted, my serve is so slow it wouldn't have damaged anything, but still … this is a tough assignment!

I stand by my statement. Public exposure is one of the best ways to get people to straighten up. Just ask yourself the question, what if everyone saw me do this? How would that feel?

Well, I can think of a couple instances—

Get your mind out of the gutter! I'm talking about day-to-day encounters, experiences, etc. You can think of it as God or a TV camera in front of you; I don't care. Now, is there anything you'd like to share?

I'm speechless!

Wow! I knew I could do it. And me without any witnesses! Perform this experiment at work today: allow a camera to follow you around.

Good grief; the viewers would die of boredom! And seriously, I'm really glad you didn't give me this assignment when I was in college. That would have been horrible!

You don't think I watched you while you were in college?

God, I hope not. I mean—

I know what you mean. People often forget God and a lot of other things when they head away from Mom and Dad for the first time.

I hope you weren't watching when I dropped that fly ball in Little League.

What is it with you and that? That happened forty years ago, and you still remember it. I promise you, you are the *only* human being that remembers that. Now would you let it go?

It was a beautiful summer night in Madison, Georgia.

Okay, I'll be your therapist! Tell the story of your losing the Little League baseball game for your team.

You spoiled the ending!

Boo hoo. Both your readers will probably forgive me!

My mommy and daddy had nice front-row seats in their lawn chairs. Get the picture (as football announcer Larry Munson used to say): My team is up by one, but the visitors have the bases loaded with two outs. A big lefty is up, so I'm a bit nervous because I'm the second baseman. As the pitcher winds up, I keep repeating, "Please don't hit that ball to me! Let's just get this out, go get our free soda, hug our parents, go home, and play kick the can with the neighbors. Or maybe some Monopoly or two-card gut. I always like taking Hunter's money." *Crack!* My reverie is disrupted by a monster high fly ball. It's way up there in the stratosphere—cardinals and blue jays are moving out of the ball's way. Even the clouds are parting. My 20–10 vision is having trouble following it—we'll blame it on that. Anyway, the runners are tearing around the bases, "touching them all" as the coaches like to say.

I'm under it—I think. It's coming down, finally! My coach is up out of his seat, ready to shake the opposing coach's hand and tell him "Better luck next time." Lawn chairs are being folded, girls are clapping, the media—who am I fooling; there was no media there! Anyway, here it comes, here it comes ...

And the stupid ball lands five yards behind me. I didn't even get a glove on it! Nothing. Come on, God; why'd you make me do that?

There you go again, blaming God. You should've caught the stupid ball. It was right to you!

Man, you sound like my coach. And the spectators. And me, for that matter.

You dropped it. You lost the game for your team.

You don't have to rub it in!

No, I did my part as far as that fly ball was concerned.

Thanks a lot!

Are you being sarcastic? You got a sympathy smooch because you dropped that fly ball. Your mother pretended not to see you up after curfew because of that fly ball. Your algebra teacher even cut you a break when grading your test. Do you think *any* of this would've happened if you had caught it?

I guess not. Here I sit, all embarrassed and chagrined.

You should be. You should've caught it. It came right to you.

Wait a second; I hate to break from sports, but what's with algebra? I mean, I'm sorry, God, but you can't add letters. You can't do it! Even you don't know what x + y equals. Can't happen!

Let's get away from this. Math teachers, for the most part, mean well. And they're a tad underpaid as compared to these athletes you want to talk about so much. So God bless teachers, math or otherwise. Now, would you get off that fly ball and get back to work and to TV cameras and to God watching you! You see my point? You've been kicking yourself for forty years for dropping a fly ball! And face it; you

never could catch a fly ball, so get over it. I didn't make you a baseball player; it's just not you. I had other ideas in mind for you.

How about co-ed softball? That's pretty fun, no?

You just like to stare at girls in their shorts, so quit changing the subject! Let me interject an analogy given to you by Wayne Dyer, one of your leading self-help gurus down there. This applies to you and *many* more. You're living your life as if you're holding on to the bars in your cell; you're gripping, clutching, agonizing, complaining. Meanwhile, to your left and right are wide open spaces. You can go around the bars easily. All you have to do is let go and move around, move on. Ironically, it really couldn't be simpler!

He said that?

Yes, and you heard it, granite head! Use some of that memory I gave you, even if you can't remember whether you washed your hair in the shower or not. By the way, this morning—you forgot. And might I suggest not going in to work with mattress marks still on your face and your hair resembling a squirrel's nest? I gave you better sense. And you once again forgot to lock your car! But let's continue. You're trying my patience, and I've got all of it in the world.

Let's talk about the Super Bowl and all those funny ads. Did you know I used to write commercials inside my head?

Yes, but I don't care. We can discuss the Super Bowl later. Or maybe we won't. I'm trying to help you here, and you just want to talk about a football game. And you're not even a Steelers or a Packers fan! I hate to be so blunt, but dude, get a life!

Okay, so I'm picturing TV cameras on me when I was back in high school trying to call a girl for a date.

Oh no, not again.

I'm in my room, all cuddled up by the phone in my pajamas. Boy am I looking and feeling like the all-time stud muffin! My untouched schoolbooks are by my bed, begging me for attention. The stereo is on WDOL—I don't know why I remember that.

Trust me again; you're the only one that does.

Anyway, the phone is beckoning me; it's curling its crooked finger and taunting me. It's just sitting there, all red and on its cradle; even the fingerprints appear to have been wiped off. It's just to my left on the end table; all I have to do is put down my unused ink pen, pick up the phone, and call the pre-memorized seven digits. That's all. I mean, after all, the groundwork had already been done.

Would you care to explain?

Of course! I'd already asked John to ask Sherry to ask Jenny to ask the girl in question if it were okay to call. She'd told Jenny to tell Sherry to tell John that the coast was clear. She would actually be waiting for my call! So there I sit, all nervous and aflutter. Is "aflutter" even a word? Well, it is now, because that's how I felt—aflutter.

Thank you for coining what was already a word, but please continue. I eagerly await your next syllable.

You just quoted the movie *Arthur*, but okay, I'll continue. Anyway, the viewers at home are on their feet, the boys are ripping me for being a spineless wimp, and the women are talking about how sweet I am to make the call. They're arguing back and forth—a point/counterpoint, if you will. Fights are breaking out on the set; it's kind of a *Jerry Springer Show* on steroids. The camera is panning in, unfortunately catching the latest pair of zits I've been harboring. They're not ready for picking yet, but perhaps God doesn't want to know that.

No, he nor anyone else, but go ahead.

Flexing both of my muscles to show off, I lift the phone off the hook while the crowd roars. Babies are hurled from the stands. The girls are getting teary-eyed. The boys are hooting and hollering at me, roaring their disapproval at my being so soft.

Excuse me, but didn't you write something about this in your first book?

Yes, but nobody read it.

Perhaps you should've learned from that, but do go on.

Quieting the crowd the way a quarterback does in a loud stadium, I begin touching the numbers—first one digit, then two, three, four. I get to six ... I can *feel* this tension and all these eyes and ears locked in on my efforts.

Might you consider that you're taking this camera thing a bit too far? Never mind, sorry to interrupt while you're sort of almost on a roll.

Almost touching the seventh and final number, my sweaty finger poised above the 7, a hush fills the nation as my digit rests less than a quarter-inch away. And ... I hang up.

You wimp!

Thanks, God, I really needed that.

You deserved that. Now, is that the end of this wonderful story?

No! I'm a persistent young man. Remember, *Columbo* is one of my many heroes.

How could I forget!

While the boys hurl objects at the camera and the girls dry their collective eyes and yell, "Oh no!" I fold my arms around my chest and regather all my God-given courage.

There you go again, blaming me!

I hear the crowd chanting, "Go! Go! Go!" Goose bumps are lining both my arms, even my legs. My hair is straightening out despite all the Vitalis I put on it. Nice invention, that stuff; what were you thinking?

Ahem.

Sorry, God, I'll go on. Talk show hosts are calculating the odds, the risks, there's a *He Said, She Said* episode breaking out. Graphs and pie charts are evident; experts are literally coming out of the woodwork.

You're hopeless.

So I would be reminded, but I'm getting to that. Literally holding my breath, I dial all seven numbers—all seven without pause!

And?

The line was busy, so I hung up and went to sleep.

That's it! You should be flogged!

So I was told the next day ... and the next. I actually took a beating, if I remember correctly. Unlike you, my memory doesn't rock.

That poor girl sat at home and waited.

A nice girl, too. Whatever happened to her?

She's married, has kids, and she's doing a lot better than you. You keep changing the subject.

What can I say? I choked under pressure! I'm glad nobody was watching me that night.

Ahem.

You keep doing that. Did you see that, too?

I was the guy in the audience throwing the chair at you. That was me. That was your sign, by the way, to make the call. You had *A* through *Y* already done for you; all you had to do was go to *Z*. And you blew it. Like I said, you should be flogged.

Well, I simply turned off my "camera" that night and put it right out of my head. I went back to ball games, science quizzes; *McCloud* episodes, and wondering what was for supper tomorrow.

Only you would take a perfect idea like public scrutiny and then get the audience involved. Might I suggest leaving the "fans" out of it?

Well, I don't want to disappoint my viewers. I mean, if they're watching, I need to put on a good show, right?

Just behave—that will be a good enough show for now. Are there any other examples you'd like to share?

Sure, could you put the cameras on a typical meeting and show the public how useless most of them are?

Now, now; not all of them are useless.

May I tell you about a few?

No, nobody wants to even go to a meeting, much less hear your report on one. Let's skip that for now.

Okay, so it's Monday and you're God and I'm trying to learn and you're telling me to act as if there is a TV camera following me about my day. You're telling me public scrutiny is the best way to solve a lot of "dirty doings." You're telling me to act as if I'm being watched. You're telling me to take you with me in my mind, not only on my "exciting" weekends but during the Monday-through-Friday hustle as well.

Exactly.

That's all well and good, but I've got mud on my pants from this morning and have to go change. Do you mind waiting outside?

A Silent Plea

Oh Great One, I appear to be stuck right now.

Then I will wait for you.

God Lends Another Hand

So what did you do this weekend with your free time?

What free time? Saturday I worked the scorer's table for three straight basketball games, from two o'clock to six thirty. It got pretty hectic. Also, I got my oil changed, had to run to the bank to make a money transfer, did some clothes shopping at Goodwill, got gas, and paid some bills. I didn't even have time to watch *Everybody Loves Raymond*.

Well, I had to invent a way to keep you sober on Saturday afternoons. Trust me, college football definitely didn't work!

Ha, very funny. I did, however, have some idle time later, but we won't go into that.

Perhaps we should. This isn't a problem most people have, but how you spend your "idle" time is very important. You need to keep your mind working in constructive ways—it will pay off in the long run. Don't just sit and let your thoughts take over. We've sort of discussed this.

What do you suggest?

Read good books, keep jogging, even do crossword puzzles, Sudoku grids, and word jumbles. Those are all good for the mind and the soul.

So I've heard. In fact, I've got one for you—this happened last weekend. You know you've had a rough night when you're working on the word jumble the next day and the letters look perfectly fine just the way they are!

Now you're being funny.

Okay, let's get back to it. God, I have a very serious question to ask you, and I mean this with every fiber in my being.

Please, go ahead.

It's Sunday as I write this. A couple of hours ago, I was sitting in a chair in Dunkin' Donuts, going through my morning ritual. My mind was in the right place; I had you there with me.

I felt that, and thanks. But continue.

Okay, I'm going through my gratitude list, and it is endless! I was thinking how grateful I was to have my health back after going through that forty-eight-hour flu virus last week. I was and am grateful that my two brothers—after a five-year feud—have reconciled and are getting along better than ever. I am grateful for the upcoming spring weather and the chance to run, play tennis, and play co-ed softball outdoors. I am grateful for my job—I am writing again. I am grateful for my finances and my health insurance. I am grateful that the cereal and the milk had just run out at the exact same time—a miracle in its own right. There you and I were, all grateful and happy. I even had this idiotic smile on my face while sitting there all by myself. People were starting to stare; one lady actually pulled her kid farther away from me while the two were standing in line.

And?

And then that bleeping, bleeping song, *Ain't No Sunshine*, played over the loudspeakers. I cannot and will not tell you how much I hate that damn song and all it stands for! The last time I heard that song was just months after my divorce. Jasper and I were out for a walk in South Florida. We were cruising around our block in North Palm Beach; it was a sunny, beautiful Sunday if there ever was one. I was still in a bit of a shock and was trying to put my life back together after Robin left—or shall I say "suggested that I leave." All of a sudden, that song came blaring out of somebody's speakers in their condo—loud and clear—piercing my innocent ears. I broke down—wept uncontrollably on the spot. I wept for my ex-wife, my bleak-looking future, my state of mind, and my total lack of motivation to do anything. In fact, I might have kept right on losing it if it hadn't been for Jasper. He actually stopped sniffing the flowers, stopped peeing on his own leg, came up to me, and jumped up onto my knee. I could actually hear him whimpering for me. That's pretty amazing when you remember that Basenjis can't bark; they rarely make any kind of noise. There he was, all cute and concerned for his master. I got down on my knees and petted him; he jumped up and put both feet on both of my shoulders and had the cutest, most worried look on his face ever. That's what finally brought me out of it.

Anyway, moving on—why in your name, after I sat there in my chair and got myself all happy and all grateful and all filled with the good spirit, why—*why, why*—did that song have to play? Why?

Sir, I have to tell you this is the most intensity I've felt coming from you in a very long time. Now, that's not saying that much—I didn't imbue you with a lot of that—but I'm being very serious when I say this.

I am intense about this! What gives? I'd worked my way—successfully, I might add—into a very happy state. The world was and is good. Even the weather, after a pretty tough winter, is getting good. The milk and cereal are both gone, but my health is back after a two-day hiatus. All is well and then—*BAM!* Why? Why? Why?

You are eagerly interested in the answer, and I am going to give it to you. I am not, contrary to popular belief, a God who will hold these truths from you. You ask, you deserve, and you will get your answer. Many of you don't think you deserve your answers, but I respectfully—always respectfully—disagree. Have you ever heard that saying, "If you want to follow me, being your friend I will help you. If you do not, I will wait until you change your mind"? It's my philosophy. Just like above, when you got stuck. I assumed you meant in your writing, but I meant it all the way around. I will wait for you. Period. End of story.

Your answer?

My answer is this: That song obviously stirs a lot of emotion in you. It should. That song appeared at the toughest of tough times for you. Let's face it—you were forty-six years old and you already had one foot in the grave. You couldn't have cared less what happened to you; you were just going to go through life letting things "happen" to you; then you were going to simply roll over and die. You, of all people, the same boy that got voted "Most Spirited" in high school, was walking around with nothing except your dog. A great dog, mind you, but still.

Hence the song. It played, and it tore and ripped into your very soul. You grieved, as you should've done earlier in the divorce—perhaps immediately. The lyrics hit home—bull's eye—and you cried.

Why bring it up again now?

Because here is the paradox, my dear friend: I want you to both remember and forget at the same time. I want you to forget for obvious reasons. I mean move on, keep living, pass Go, collect what's yours,

and keep cruising. On the other hand, I always want you to remember so you will continue to be grateful for how far you've come. If I don't send you reminders, the tendency is to repeat yourself, to go back to your same mistakes. I *want* you to hear that song, and when you do, I want you to pat yourself on the back, not cry. I want you to be grateful for how good things are now, for all that you've accomplished in getting out of the grave, for the fact that you are living again, a caring, breathing, tax-paying human who cares.

In short, the next time you hear that song, instead of getting mad, instead of doubling over, instead of missing your wife and your dog, I want you to look up at me and smile. I want you to express joy in your almost literally escaping your own physical death as well as your mental one.

You're saying I actually have to like that song?

No, just like what it stands for to you. Smile and give thanks. You've come a long way. So hear this: Maybe a year or two down the road, definitely when you least expect it, you will hear it again. You might be driving your kids back from tennis or a cross-country meet. You might be working the word jumble and trying to un-jumble the letters "NIVTNE" to form a word. You might be successfully or unsuccessfully working the *USA Today* crossword puzzle. Anyway, you will hear it all, but this time, instead of focusing on the "Ain't No Sunshine When She's Gone" part, focus on the part where the singer keeps saying, "I know, I know, I know, I know, I know." Remember that part? That's the part I want you to keep in your soul. Because now you do know. You know you are to remember that period of your life and you are to forget it. Remember to listen. Smile at me; don't raise your tiny fists. Yes, I took you practically to hell, and I was with you every step of the way while you came back. In a way, it would actually fit if you did begin liking that song, but I'll never mess with your free will.

I must say that in hearing it this morning, it actually gave me a physical shock—and I couldn't figure out for the life of me why. Thanks for that; it actually makes sense. Don't get me wrong; I'm not going out to buy the CD or anything. But I'll at least try to have a new appreciation for that song. See, I did it! I didn't write "that damn song"; I simply said "that song." I'm getting better already.

That's the idea, isn't it?

That's what they say, whoever "they" are. But now—once again—it's time to lighten things up a bit.

Great, hit me with some Facebook wisdom. Or read me a quote. Or tell me about one of your dates in high school or college. Doesn't matter, I laugh in all cases.

Okay, how's this one: in dog beers, I've only had one!

It really figures you'd like that one!

To quote from *Columbo*, let's see now, where were we?

You just had a conniption over that song. Let's continue with that day: how did things go after the Dunkin' Donuts incident?

I didn't recover until writing this and getting your answer. I actually couldn't wait to get to my keyboard to see what you had to say. I think I actually broke about three traffic laws getting there, but I'll just pretend you and the cops didn't see that.

Fortunately for you, the cops didn't. They had other pressing matters in Sandy Springs. You're welcome, by the way. Now did you have a good rest of the weekend? Did you stay out of trouble?

Absolutely. I got very little work done but consulted with God most of the day on my Apple computer here in Sandy Springs—the last place you'd ever look. Would you have talked to me if I were on a PC, or are you an Apple guy—or do you care? I'm partial to Royal typewriters myself, but they've pretty much gone by way of the Dunlop tennis rackets with the two-handed grips. Great rackets, by the way, but who's counting? Did you know my father took one of my old broken ones and made a clock out of it—even put the numbers fifteen, thirty, and forty on it, for tennis' sake. It was pretty innovative. We hung it in our den for years before—

Excuse me.

Sorry.

Let's move on. The clock was nice; it was some of his finer work. But let's move on to some more pressing issues. Don't you want to talk about job interviews, the workforce, money and the economy, Mother Nature and how you guys are screwing her all up, education, health, and just a few of the finer issues of your time?

Sure, that'd be great, but could you hang on a second? A *How I Met Your Mother* marathon is coming on the Chicago channel right now. I should be with you in about two or two and a half hours.

You're hopeless!

God Goes to Jail

This time it's my turn to report to you.

What's up? What happened?

I got arrested today.

God got arrested! What in the world did you do? How could God possibly get arrested?

Since you asked … your cell phone rang at six fifteen this morning—sick teacher. I felt that you've been doing a bang-up job as substitute teacher coordinator, and I felt you needed your rest.

Thank you.

You're welcome. So I took the call. I didn't have the heart to wake you. There you were, enjoying a five-star drool-inducing slumber, having peaceful dreams that I won't mention, and I just couldn't shake you. So I took the call. One of your upper school teachers is down with the flu, bless his heart, and he requested a sub. Instead of having you wake up and start calling people, I took it upon myself to be the sub.

You went to school?

Yes—I went in disguised as Allen Cross, history sub.

Cute.

I thought so. Anyway, I borrowed your green pants; hope you don't mind. Regardless, I obeyed the "business casual" dress code—I had on your green khakis, a collared shirt—no hat, by the way—and loafers. I was looking pretty collegiate, if I say so myself.

This is good. I got in trouble once after coming into school after tennis in my warm-up suit. "This isn't a locker room," I was told. Terribly embarrassing. Still, please continue. I'm dying to hear how God got arrested.

I walked into class and decided we were going to start the day in prayer.

You didn't.

Oh, I did. I requested all my cute loved ones to bow their little heads and say a prayer to whatever God they believed in. I requested they pray for peace and a life of service, joy, love, and gratitude. I didn't even make them do it in God's name. After all, it was a pretty diverse class; there were a couple Buddhists in there. Still, I didn't differentiate.

What happened?

One of the students said, "Who are you to make us do this?"

I replied by saying, "You wouldn't believe me if I told you!" Besides, who was going to get them in trouble anyway, and why? I told him his day would probably be at least 10 percent better if he started it every morning in some type of prayer. You humans are funny; you're always

too "busy." Little do you know how much I could help you with your busyness if you'd just let me!

Okay, so they prayed. Then what?

Then I got called in to the principal's office!

Really? You got reported!

Yes, the little guy called his mother, who called her husband, who called the head of school. I was sitting in his office before third period.

What did he say?

He had me show him my ID, first of all. Now, I don't have any ID that says "Allen Cross" on it. My ID is simple—it simply reads "God." There's no job title under my name. I mean, I figure just "God" should be enough, don't you think? And now you see why I don't come down here disguised as a human! You people want me to show up, and then when I do, I get arrested and called a crackpot! Do you believe that? I'm trying to put some fresh air into our schools, and I'm called names and ridiculed.

As soon as they saw my ID, that man went to his cell phone and called security on me. Security didn't say a word to me; just walked up, frisked me and put me in handcuffs. He asked me where my wallet and keys were, but I'd already made them disappear. I mean, what car did he think God drove to school in? I'll admit, I am partial to Hondas because of their gas mileage and dependability, but there are a lot of good cars out there.

So there he is, asking me for my "God" ID and searching me for a cell phone or anything that would make me, in his mind, human. There I was, being all polite and being all godlike and he was reading me my rights. Get this: *he* was telling *me* that I should remain silent. *He* was telling *me* that anything I said could be used against me in a

court of law. I'm the good book they swear to when they take the stand in the first place! Don't you see the sad humor in this? All the while, he had this funny look on his face while he was arresting me. He knew something was wrong—I made sure of it! Something just felt a little "off" to him about what he was doing. Still, he had a job to do, and in this time of economic crisis, he didn't want to lose it—even if he did have to arrest God to keep it. Now there's another irony—he had to arrest God to keep his job!

Then what happened?

I was in handcuffs and in the back of the paddy wagon. I was off to the gray bar hotel, if you'll pardon the expression. Instead of God, I was about to become prisoner #32893. Now get this, when they put me in my cell, they handed me a Bible! The guys says to me, "Read this; it might do you some good."

What did you say to that?

I just said, "I will read it, so help me me." After all, he, too, was only doing his job. So I was locked in a small cell, and my "roommate" was on his hands and knees in prayer. I hated to interrupt his prayer, but he was going about it all the wrong way. He was leaving too much up to me and not taking appropriate action himself; I had to interrupt. So I did; I said, "Excuse me, I'm right here!"

What did he say to that?

He got really mad! Told me to shut the bleep up while he was trying to pray. And get this—he actually told me he had better people to be talking to at the moment. Then he pointed up to the sky. Why do people always do that? Why don't they point south, east, or west? Or like you said, how do you people think you can have north, south, east, and west when the world is round?

What did you do?

I walked over and tapped him on the shoulder. I had to—his prayers were so ... desperate and without passion. The man was already giving up! Don't you sports nuts remember the famous Jim Valvano speech, "Never give up!" That was a great speech! I gave him that idea. He rocked that night; people still listen to that speech on YouTube and all those other Internet places, and they should. He was inspiring! I blessed that man with passion! But I digress.

Anyway, I tapped him on the shoulder and handed him my business card—you know—the one that has just "God" written on it. I wish you could've seen the look in that man's eyes. I swear they went circular on me—through, inside, above, and around his head. He felt something, but he didn't believe it, so he threw my business card at me and called me a crackpot. Do you believe it? Second time in one day I was called a crackpot. What is it with you humans? You beg and beg and beg me to come down here—either that or send my son. Then, when I do it, I'm tossed in a prison and mocked! And look what you've already done to my son! You think I'm going to send my own precious son down here again anytime soon? Are you kidding? Would *you* let your son go through that? Twice? Who are we kidding here?

What did the prisoner say?

He didn't say anything for a long while. He had this stressed but deep look on his face, if that makes any sense. He kept looking at me and the card, which I thought was odd. I mean, I don't have my picture on there or anything. Why was I so crazy to think that just "God" should be sufficient on my business card? Do I need a job title or a work extension? Do I have to have a cell phone number and an e-mail address? Do I really? If you want me, just get quiet for a few moments and call—no phone number required, thank you very much. No offense to iPhones and BlackBerrys, mind you; I'm sure they've been coming in good use down there, especially among teenagers—

though don't get me started on texting while driving. Did you read that bumper sticker: "Honk if you love Jesus. Text while driving if you want to meet him really soon!"

Anyway, can you picture God making a call on a BlackBerry? I can't. Just the thought of it makes me laugh. But back to the prisoner. Finally he says to me, "I'm a printer; I could have one of these cards made for less than two bucks!"

"But it wouldn't be genuine!" I said back, a big, welcoming smile on my face. "And by the way, quit praying so much for other people to do this and do that. It's time for *you* to get going. You're relying on—and then getting too frustrated with—other people when it is *you* who can start changing your life around. Leave them alone; they're fighting their own battles. And quit asking me to forgive you. I forgive you; now let's work on you getting some of your fellow humans to forgive you. They're the ones you're going to be spending the rest of your life with—you hope.

You can be pretty tough sometimes, you know that?

I *have* to be pretty tough sometimes, oddly enough, even with the devoutly religious. I've instilled the power in them; go use it! I can't do everything. Better yet, I don't *have* to do everything—I've given *you* people many powers. I've given you a very powerful mind. If only you knew how powerful your minds were! That is one of my greatest wishes to you humans—that you realize how powerful you really are. Granted, you need direction often, but you yourself could do so much, and all I would have to do would be sit, watch, and cheer you on. It'd be my own version of college football Saturdays. Surely you can relate to that, right?

Oh yes, college football rocks! Go Dawgs! Sorry, go on with your story. I still can't believe God spent time in jail.

Think again, my good son. I'm in jail all the time. That's probably where I'm called on the most—there and in the end zone. And soccer players are getting pretty needy, too, but never mind that. I've done my best work in jail—I just didn't plan on wearing a uniform and working from the inside. I felt like *Brubaker*—and I know you saw that movie.

Pretty obscure, but go ahead.

The prisoner stood up; I thought at first he was going to hit me. Then a very confused look crossed his face. His eyebrows shot upward and his nose curled. He was thinking of what I just told him, and he was wondering how in the world I knew what he was praying about. He literally couldn't figure out how to proceed—like the bully who wants to hit someone but is quickly going over the consequences in his cute little head—should I or shouldn't I? Then he said, "If you're God, what in the world are you doing in here?"

"You called on me, didn't you?" I said. "I heard you! I was listening. Here I am. You have my full, rapt attention."

He actually curled up his fist after that one—he really *was* going to have a go at me. I should've warned him—I do know martial arts. Well actually, I sort of invented martial arts, but that's beside the point. So I simply told him, "If you strike me, that will only add time to your sentence—six months and twenty-eight days, to be exact. And you're due out of here in two years. Actually, you don't know this, but you'll be out in just nineteen months for good behavior. Do you really want to screw that up?

"How the hell do you know that?" he said.

"I told you; I'm God! I actually know everything!"

"Well if you're so smart, how come you're in this cell with me, wearing prison clothes and looking like a normal man?"

"Actually, I look like a substitute teacher. My name was Allen Cross, and I subbed today in history at this private school. I tried to say a prayer, got called to the principal's office, got myself arrested; now here I am! Voila!"

"God got arrested. And I'm supposed to believe that? They'll lock me up for a lot longer than nineteen months if I go spouting this off! I'll be in solitary before lunch. And trust me, God, you don't want to spend a second in solitary.

"Been there, though I don't really understand the concept. It wasn't me who invented that; I'm going to put that one off on you silly humans. I'll chalk it up as yet another dumb idea that came from a staff meeting, and we'll let it go at that.

He walked closer to me then. He was sizing me up, wondering if he could "take me," so to speak. You humans are funny about this fighting thing. Don't you realize? Fighting isn't a sport; it's a hormone problem! It was one of my greatest mistakes! You people actually pay money to watch people in a cage beat each other up and then you call yourselves civilized! How can you do that? Have you not advanced any further than that after more than two thousand years? Have you really not? See! You're complaining from having to listen to *Ain't No Sunshine* and getting mad about it, how do you think I feel? I see people jumping up and down screaming over people beating each other up, and I'm supposed to feel happy! Am I really? And how would you like it if somebody popped you in the head and thousands upon thousands of people cheered about it? Can't you people get it? What is it going to take?

You sound very passionate about this.

I *am* very passionate about this, and I still don't get it! And I'm God! I'm supposed to get everything! I should've never invented confusion, but that's mostly what I get sometimes. Remember that song from years ago, *Ball of Confusion*? The songwriter wasn't very far off. I'm glad he put my idea into existence, because as he said, "that's what the world is today."

Okay, so the prisoner was sizing you up, considering beating God to a pulp. Even saying that sounds terribly wrong somehow, but go ahead.

"You don't know what confusion means!" the guy said. "My whole life is confusion. If you're God, why don't you fix it?"

"My point is, why don't you?" I said to the guy. "You ignore my signs because of your foolish ego, you don't listen to your own good sense, you go against your better judgment time and again, and now you're here not only not listening to me, but also wanting to beat me up! And I'm the one that's been sending you the proper road signs to begin with. Don't you people ever get it?"

What did he say to that?

He actually started laughing, but it wasn't a real laugh, if you know what I mean. He was laughing more in desperation; more of a sense of "what do I have to lose by listening to this guy" type of thing. It wasn't sincere, let's put it that way! I could almost literally see the wheels spinning in his head—he came so close to doing the right thing. However—and this is why he's in jail in the first place—he listened to his ego instead of listening to his good sense. He pushed me aside, walked to the end of his cell, and started yelling to his cellmates. "Hey everybody, I've got God in here as my roommate. He's here in jail, stopping in to save the world. I'm serious! This guy thinks he's God!"

Within seconds, the place went crazy. Prisoners walked to the bars, yelling and hollering. "Hey God, come be my lawyer. I got screwed the first time!" "Hey God, get me out of here; I was framed!" "God, how come you're in here? Was God a bad boy?"

On and on it went, and it only got louder. Soon the whole place erupted—it seemed like every cell had both prisoners standing at the bars screaming at me. All of them! My cellmate just stood there laughing.

What did you do?

I walked up and got right in his face and said, "What you just did is the sole and the soul reason you're in here in the first place. You almost listened to your good sense; then your big ego got in the way. Instead of hearing my voice, you chose to ignore it. *This* is why you're here. You're actually one of the lucky ones, do you know that? After all, your life isn't over; you're not in for life. You actually have a chance of making a go of it once you get out of here."

"What the hell do you know?" he said, still acting tough.

"A lot more than you'll ever know, and I'm still trying to help you regardless. So quit praying to me for forgiveness. I forgive you; enough already. How about trying to make things right with the humans you have wronged—your loved ones and the entire destructive ripple you have caused. Get *them* to forgive you; they're the ones that count right now. I'm already on your side. Now start listening, and quit acting like a jerk!

Wow, God got tough!

Sometimes I have to, as I've said. You people get sign after sign— not just from eight-track tape players by the way—and you still don't listen. Then you beg me and blame me once you're in trouble. That guy knows better—he always has! Again, "always" is one and two words. It's so frustrating.

Go on with your story.

About that time, one of the screws came out and let me go. He said the charges were dropped and I was free to go. He said it with a smirk on his face: "God, you may go." He then started laughing, and the entire gated community laughed with him. They got a big kick out of me getting arrested. You have to admit, it was quite an irony.

What was?

Well, I got thrown out of the public and into the jail; then I got thrown out of the jail that I got thrown into in the first place. I can't go anywhere down here with you humans!

Never thought of it like that.

Anyway, there I was without my business casual uniform on—all dressed up and no place to go. As I walked down the aisle, some of the guys were trying to touch me, all the while yelling, "Heal me, Lord! Come on, just one touch! Get me out of this place." It went on like that every step of the way, from the end of my cellblock all the way to the front. One guy actually grabbed my sleeve and tore it; the guard threatened to make me pay for it. He actually switched sides with me for protection; that was nice of him, though he did it more to be mean to the prisoners than to be nice to me. He's a hard guy, that guard. Then again, most of them have to be, though many take it too far.

What a story!

Glad you liked it. Now I've got to get back there in spirit; you'll have to excuse me.

Where are you going?

Some of them in jail actually believed it was me, though they didn't have the guts to admit it. I'm going back. A lot of the inmates are busy calling my name. Still, stay in touch with me; we'll talk. And by the way, if you ever need another sub, Allen Cross is at your service!

Oh dear.

An Eerie "Coincidence"

This is almost too corny to put in here.

What is?

What happened to me today at school. If I were reading this, I wouldn't believe it.

You're not supposed to believe everything you read—especially nowadays.

Still, can I promise to God this is true?

Yes, you can promise to me it's true. What happened?

I was in class today, subbing in science. That's kind of funny in itself. Still, I was sitting at the front of the room, disguised as an authority figure—had it down to a science. Had my glasses on, my arms on the desk, a coffee mug next to me—you'd have been proud.

You can't fool me.

Of course not, but other people might've fallen for it.

So what happened?

A kid in the back—Zach Waldron is his name, to be exact—started singing.

So?

So he was singing *Ain't No Sunshine*!

I don't even believe it, and I'm God!

I asked him why he was singing that. I mean, that song was written *way* before he was even born.

What'd he say?

He said the upper school chorus is performing that song this month, in concert.

That is weird.

For the record, he also said he hated the song. I just wanted to throw that in.

That's not the question.

What's the question?

The question is, how did you react to it this time? Did you break down? Double over? Need your dog to run over and help? Did you remember? Did you use it as a positive lesson?

Of course! Or, to quote from the song again: "I know, I know, I know, I know …"

Okay, let's move on to more believable stuff.

You're the boss.

Exactly. Now please remember that. Spread the word, even.

God, Author Go on Spring Break

Are you back? Tell me about your spring break. Where'd you go? What'd you do?

I find it interesting that God asks me what I did and where I went. And I'm doubly happy to report that I not only took you with me, but also that I've written you up a full report. And my full apologies go out to you if you're not a baseball fan.

Oh, I'm a fan—baseball is probably one of the purest games there is. In fact, the few changes they've made over the years haven't necessarily been good ones. That's a game that has never needed much adjusting.

You mean changes like the designated hitter and whoever wins the All-Star game gets the host the World Series.

That is *exactly* what I'm talking about. Enough, though; let's get to your report. And thank you, by the way, for thinking of me while you were enjoying your fun in the sun/baseball/spring break.

You're welcome. Here goes:

Meditations from North Florida

It's that time again, spring break—a week off. Our kids will empty out of our buildings and into airports faster than I can nuke a pizza. They will head to chalets, town houses, beaches, foreign countries—all that and then some. For this journalist, who will for the first time attempt to be a photojournalist, it's the annual travels with the varsity baseball team—a four-game "spring training" tour of North Florida. For those of you who aren't new to this, you may be familiar with former titles. There was "On the Road with the Defending State Champs" (2008), "The Cocoa Chronicles" (don't remember the year), and "Fear and Loathing in North Florida," and I think I'm forgetting one. Returning to the present, we're not going to call this one "Fear and Loathing, Part II," even though we're going to the same places as last year. After all, I hate sequels (James Bond movies notwithstanding). We'll settle for "Meditations from North Florida," since (1) it's different and (2) meditation is the most underrated thing ever.

What follows is my transformation from PR man/substitute teacher/tennis coach to "bat boy," where I will loiter in the HI dugouts, spit sunflower seeds, contribute to gossip, and call kids by their nicknames. And who knows, if the wind is blowing right (or if the coaches are in a really good mood), I might even shag some flies during batting practice. Coaches, players, and even parents may or may not be interviewed, games will be written up, and basically, the show will go on.

A note: I won't be insulted if you don't have the time to read all this. Perhaps I should applaud you for saving the time. After all, taxes are due, March Madness is here in more ways than one, and chores simply can't wait.

If you have the time, however, please join me in Florida. Adventures with high school kids—well written or not—are more often than not priceless. I will not change names; I believe firmly in the innocence of our kids, and I'll be as direct as possible. After all, this is a society of lazy readers. And as it happens, I am a lazy writer.

Let's move on. It's warm out, the bell just rang, releasing us into the unsuspecting public, and I could've sworn I just heard an umpire yell, "Play Ball!"

Tuesday, March 6

ATLANTA to SHELLMAN BLUFF—Eight coaches and a journalist convene onto South Campus, Holy Innocents', USA. It is 4:45 a.m.; do you know where your baseball team is? Yes, they're asleep—the lucky ones—while we're standing in the freezing cold, holding coffee cups as if for life support, trying to wipe off the mattress marks still etched onto our faces. Yes, waking up is hard to do and no one is doing it except for Assistant Coach Dan Healy. His coffee apparently has already worked its magic and elevated his spirits; he's laughing, loading vans, dreaming of the days ahead in paradise. Rumor has it he marked these days on a calendar in his office during January—last January—and the thoughts of the days ahead and baseball have him energetic way too early. Normally I avoid "morning people," but I force myself to stand near him, as if trying to catch whatever he has. His liveliness and Deal's agenda eventually work their way into my system. To paraphrase: Day number one—before baseball—let there be golf!

Unlike the drama of three years ago where the front right tire blew in Macon, the drive is nothing but "White Line Fever" on the freeways—quick, painless—with a brief stop at McDonald's for a nasty Egg McMuffin. Unfortunately for the employees at Sapelo

Hammock Golf Course in Shellman Bluff, Georgia (wherever that
is), we make it in less than five hours and with time to spare.

A few words about golf and then we'll move on. After all,
it's the kids' world, so I won't spend too many words on the
adults. There are eight coaches golfing—I myself opt out due to
sanity. After all, the sport is about six holes too long, and running
into snakes while searching for golf balls in the woods no longer
appeals to me. In the words of Jack Nicholson, "I'd rather stick
needles in my eye."

For the baseball staff, however, this is serious. Today's adventure
will pit the four varsity coaches against the JV/middle school staff.
In translation, it is Dylan Deal, Jay Hood (Hoodie), Cameron
Lane, and Healy against Marshall Gaines, Ben DeSantis, Bill
Cefaratti, and Bert Olsen. Bets are made—something about
taking the other's firstborn or doing the other's laundry for a year,
but maybe I'm exaggerating a bit. (I'll do that a couple of times in
this piece. Just go with it for effect).

I will give you the rumors I heard while compiling the scores;
you can decide if I'm lying or not: One of Cefaratti's drives may
or may not have killed a duck. Bert sliced it so badly that when he
teed off, the deer wandered out of the woods and into the fairways.
Deal, who actually hit it backward two years in a row (and I'm
not kidding), was a putting machine. Hoodie ripped the tar out
of the ball, often and almost always. It took Gaines a couple holes
to get going—I detected anger early—but apparently he got over
it and played well.

The varsity team won by a stroke. The media was alerted. The
highlight for this journalist was Hole 12. After all, it was there we
saw an alligator—about three feet long or so. "Should we draw
straws to see who gets to wrestle it?" Deal said.

Not being good at mixed martial arts—actually considering the whole business a hormone problem rather than a sport—I prayed I would get the long straw. I didn't. Luckily, the alligator swam off before I could make my attack. Yes, there is a God.

Hands were shaken, war stories were told in the clubhouse about the misadventures, pretzels were destroyed with passion, and it was back into vans 19 and 21.

SHELLMAN BLUFF to DARIEN—Through a contact of Gaines, we stay in a very large mansion in Darien that overlooks the marshes and the sunset. Upon casing the joint, I figure the place can hold plus or minus 264 people—270 if you include the couches.

Despite this, we still manage to step all over each other as we again draw straws to see who gets to attack the two showers. Once again I lose—I draw the number-eight position. To put it briefly, my shower is so cold that I'm in and out of there faster than a politician can tell a lie. I am dirty, I am tired, and I miss my home and reruns of *The Big Bang Theory*. But baseball awaits; therefore, I am happy.

Off we go to invade some place called Skippers for dinner.

It's a party of ten on the porch—they always put my parties out on the porch—and before this night is over, our waitress perhaps wants to wrestle us. Still, we are behaved—not counting the golf lies. Some of the coaches find a place to play cornhole or bocci ball or something or other. They get passionate out there. In fact, they use not only the playing field, but include half the restaurant as their course. To use golf terms, let's just say they "played through" a couple of times.

Still, no harm, no foul. The only damage of the night is that this journalist accidentally parked one of the vans in the wrong driveway back at the house. I say my prayers in solemn hope that the people I blocked in have no life, nowhere to go after 8:00 p.m., no emergencies. God hears my prayer, and I can almost swear I hear Him call me an idiot. Still, I mean well. That counts for something.

We return to the house for friendly cards and conversation. Good night, and may the peace be with us.

Wednesday, March 7

DARIEN to JACKSONVILLE—I offer a one-word piece of advice for any traveler who is considering breakfast at the local Waffle House in Darien, Georgia: don't! The only other comment I wish to impart is that the coffee is safe—please forego the rest of the menu.

The morning is I-95 down to Jacksonville, where we meet the team in the hotel at the Fairfield Inn & Suites and head off to the practice fields for a couple of hours. We're only thirty minutes behind schedule—I choose to blame that on the Waffle House, but who's counting.

It's good to be on the field with the team. Speaking of on the field, there's a Toronto Blue Jays scout here, videotaping Skye Bolt as he takes BP. This will be a frequent scene as we go through this year. We send Skye good vibes as he rips ropes into all fields. May the scout be impressed and spread the word.

Today's starting pitcher is Will Small. You can always spot the starter, as he's usually the one off to the side, sitting alone, looking as if he got slapped by his mother, best friend, and girlfriend all during study hall.

"I don't have any set routine," Small says while taking in the practice. "I just listen to my music. I even clown around a little and play some jokes on people." He puts his music back in, focuses. I choose to leave him alone.

After barbeque at a place called Gator something or other, it's off to the field. It's a 4:00 p.m. game, and the honorable Coach Dylan Deal calls his players over.

"This is our sanctuary. Let's have some fun, make decisions and take care of each other. Is there anywhere else you want to be?" A chorus of "No!" rings through the air, the field is taken, and I now shoot you over to the HIES website.

Bears Edge Eagle View 6-5

3/7

JACKSONVILLE - Powered by the bats of **Jake Maziar** and **Skye Bolt**, the HI baseball team began its "Spring Training" Wednesday afternoon with a 6-5 win over Eagle View Academy at Eagle View. Coach **Dylan Deal's** team will continue its tour of North Florida tomorrow (Thursday), with a 6 p.m. game against Bolles of Jacksonville before traveling across the state for two games in Gainesville.

Maziar went 2-for-4 on the day with a double, a homer and four RBI, while Bolt (2-for-3) doubled, homered and brought in two. "I was just seeing it well up there," Maziar said. "Also, I've got some reliable guys in front of me who kept getting on base." The senior catcher also threw out a runner trying to steal third which thwarted a potential Warrior rally in the later innings.

"I just relaxed and let the game come to me," Bolt added. "Plus, it's sunny and 75 degrees down in Florida which makes it a lot of fun to play baseball."

While the two provided the offensive heroics, it was as simple as one-two-three on the mound as **Will Small, Alec Bicknese** and

Charles Link got the job done. Small got the win, going four innings, allowing three runs and striking out four. Bicknese was the set up man - the junior threw two scoreless innings and fanned one while Link hung on for the save in the seventh.

"I was locating my fastball pretty well and my changeup was working," Small summarized.

The Bears scored a single run in the first, three in the third and single runs in the sixth and seventh. Small factored in in the first inning scoring as he led off the game with an infield hit. After **Sam Lukens** sacrificed him over, Bolt doubled him home making it 1-0 Bears.

The third was HI's biggest frame, as Maziar came up with the bases loaded and delivered a bases-clearing double into the gap. **Keller Latty** started it off with an infield single, Small reached by a fielder's choice and Bolt was intentionally walked to set the table for Maziar.

Maziar hit a solo homer in the sixth over the right-center wall and Bolt went yard over left-center in the final frame. The Bears collected seven hits in the effort.

"The pitchers did a great job today," Deal said after the game. "The defense also played well. We manufactured some runs early; we need to be able to count on that from players 1-through-9 in the lineup."

With the victory, the Bears are now 3-1 on the season. After returning from Florida Saturday afternoon/evening, HI returns to action Monday at home against Wesleyan.

Thirty-three baseball personnel plus parents invade a steak house after the game. It's always priceless seeing the manager's face when a party of thirty-three-plus walk in—it's an expression of shock mixed with the "I'm about to pass a kidney stone" look.

Regardless, the food rocked. Thanks to Mr. Voyles for treating us.

All is relatively quiet back at the hotel. I fall asleep to *Seinfeld*.

Thursday, March 8

Some random comments heard, shared, or made up while at breakfast:

- Marshall Gaines went to the pier this morning and caught seven fish—four whiting and three sand perch.
- Peyton Manning and the Indianapolis Colts are parting ways after fourteen years.
- Cefaratti owns his own bowling ball and almost brought it on this trip.
- And last but not least, in the barbaric times of cock fighting, owners put cayenne pepper on the bird's front side to make it more aggressive. Would that work for my cross-country team?

We're sitting at the hotel during the morning hours. It is game day. The problem is, it is only 10:00 a.m. and the game's not until 6:00 p.m. What to do all day? Ready … go!

Mitchell Davis: I play Xbox and cards and hack into other people's Facebook accounts.

Sam Lukens: I don't do anything weird; I just wake up early, eat a big breakfast, and watch about an hour of TV. I don't do lunch on game days.

Will Small: I buy lotto tickets.

Ben DeSantis ran for an hour.

Jake Maziar: I play Xbox, go for a light jog, and maybe do some push-ups and sit-ups.

Tal Kelsey: I relax and try not to spend all my energy. I just try to have some fun and not worry too much about the game.

Cameron Lane graded papers.

The journalist sweated out prior seafood dinners with a run on the treadmill.

And finally, this piece would be remiss if Hoodie weren't asked this question. After all, with great high school careers in Tennessee and then Georgia Tech before a stint in the big leagues in the Angels organization, who else would know more about killing time before a game?

"I have routines as a player that carried over into coaching. There's lots of card playing in hotel rooms. I would always get my uniform out—piece-by-piece—and then get it situated on the bed where I could pack it later. Certain things would have to be packed a certain way; I have a ritual where you put a certain sock on first, then the other.

"A couple of hours before the game, I'd veg in the room and chew on some sunflower seeds—get my mind on the game. I'd go through the whole game in my head—situations both offensively and defensively.

"Now, as a coach, I go through it on two levels. First, I try to think like a player so it prepares me as a coach. Second, I go through all of our players' at bats from the night before—what adjustments need to be made? Do we need to change their approach?

"Finally, on rainy days we'd roll up tube socks and play soft toss back in the room. We'd hit the socks up against the wall. We'd get our swings in, particularly since obviously we weren't going to get any at bats that day."

Coach Deal also has his own solution for what to do on the big day: load up all the kids and take them bowling!

So off we go. Two vans, crammed with kids, golf clubs, and bags, minus Cefaratti's bowling ball, head to the lanes. It's usually the kids against the coaches—smack talking included—and today is no exception.

Since I'm now tired of typing, I take you to our bowling journalist for a recap of today's events at the local lanes.

"It was the birthday boy—Hoodie—who ruled the day on the lanes, picking up the highest two scores with a 159 and a 182. Gaines had a turkey—that's three strikes in a row, for those of you scoring at home. Mitchell Davis rolled a 131, but that's a random fact, and I don't know why I'm including it.

Still, in recapping this day, I ask you to close your eyes and picture Coach Dylan Deal with a bowling ball in his hand, about to make his approach. Picture Chris Farley in the movie *Tommy Boy*. Picture Farley/Deal screaming as he runs down the lane—the ball traveling somewhere around 180 miles per hour with gusts up to 220. Picture the ball flying about two-thirds of the way down the lane before it ever hits, then see it bouncing over the pins, hitting the back wall and bouncing back onto the lane. (I'm lying again; go with it). And finally, picture the bowling lane manager getting *very* nervous every time it's Deal's turn to bowl.

You might not get a good picture in your heads, ladies and gentlemen, but I myself am laughing very hard. Back to you, Dunn."

Tonight's test is a tough one—the Bolles Bulldogs were back-to-back state champions in 2009 and 2010, and they're throwing their ace against us—some stud muffin named Hayden Hurst. He supposedly runs it up there around 90–92 mph, so the stage is set.

Scouts are here from the Tigers and, I think, the Mets. It's a beautiful night for baseball. And once again, we go to the website:

Bears Beat Bolles in Dramatic Fashion

3/8
   With the game deadlocked at 2 in the top of the seventh, Holy Innocents' catcher **Jake Maziar** drilled a three-run homer over the left-centerfield fence to help lift the Bears to a nail-biting 5-2 win over

a good Bolles School team Thursday night at Bolles. With the victory, Coach **Dylan Deal's** squad lifted its record to 4-1 and will now travel across the state to Gainesville for two more "Spring Training" games - a 6 p.m. Friday contest against Gainesville High and a 1 p.m. Saturday date with Buchholz High.

In the pivotal final inning, **Keller Latty** led off with a single and **Will Small** bunted him over. After **Skye Bolt** was intentionally walked, Maziar came to the plate and delivered the heroics.

"I just tried to relax up there, especially since I had such a bad approach the at-bat before," Maziar said. "Basically I was just trying to do a job."

"This was a great win," Deal added. "I was proud of the fight we showed. That's a good team we just beat; we did a great job of scrapping and battling. We got the bunts down when we needed to and got some great pitching."

The great pitching came from **Ed Voyles** and **Alec Bicknese;** HI also got some huge defensive plays throughout the game. Voyles went 4 1/3 innings, struck out six and allowed only one run; Bicknese got the win, throwing 2 2/3, fanning four and allowing an unearned run.

"My changeup kept them off balance so I just worked off of that," Voyles said.

"I felt I was snapping off my curve pretty good and they never adjusted," Bicknese added. Bicknese pitched out of a 1-out, bases loaded jam in the fifth by striking out the next two batters.

Besides the work on the hill, perhaps the biggest defensive play came in the bottom of the sixth with the score at 2-2. The Bulldogs, with a runner on second and two outs, delivered a single to Bolt in centerfield. Bolt, with professional scouts watching from the stands, delivered a perfect strike to Maziar at home to gun down the would-be go-ahead run from Bolles.

"I trusted my arm; I knew I could get it there," Bolt said. "My only concern was throwing it up the line, not behind the plate." Maziar, from his end, blocked the plate perfectly to keep the game tied for the moment.

In the early innings, **Tal Kelsey** came up big several times with the glove at short, while Maziar - for the second night in a row - gunned down a would-be base stealer.

The Bears found themselves down 1-0 after a first inning homer, but tied the game in the top of the fourth when Bolt led off with a walk and stole second. After taking third on a deep fly out by Maziar, Bolt was then balked home by the Bulldogs' pitcher.

HI took a 2-1 lead in the fifth; Latty led off the frame with a walk. He took second on a wild pitch, was bunted over to third by Small and scored on another wild pitch. Bolles tied the game in the bottom of the sixth on an unearned run.

Deal's squad collected four hits; **Sam Lukens** was 1-for-4 with a double, Maziar went 2-for-4 for the second straight night and Latty was 1-for-2 with a single. Small laid down two perfect sacrifice bunts; **Sam Jokerst** also delivered a timely bunt. Latty and Bolt both scored two runs.

Back at the hotel, Hoodie said, "That was the most exciting game I've been a part of since the state championship game of 2007."

"It was a playoff atmosphere," Jim Voyles said, chiming in. "The game was close, and there was a lot of back-and-forth going on."

"That was the best game I've ever played in at HI," Lukens said.

Perhaps this puts it in perspective: Alec Bicknese, normally a stoic young lad, stormed off the field after getting out of his bases-loaded, one-out jam. After slamming his glove on the bench, Bicknese ran poles with the substitutes even though he was still in the game.

"I had to keep moving," he says with a smile. "The adrenaline was up, and the extra movement helped."

And to cap off this night, the words of Coach Deal sum things up rather nicely: "It's really nice to see the *other* team getting chewed out after the games."

Good night. We're 2–0 on the trip. Don't mess with a winning streak. Don't shave. Keep doing what you're doing. Until tomorrow ...

Friday, March 9

Off to the pier we go for a morning of clearing our heads. Bert, Deal, Gaines, Hoodie, and Cefaratti catch some fish and throw them back. This journalist runs five miles, still buzzing about last night's game.

Back at the hotel, Carter Brehm sits in the lobby. Rumor has it he might get an inning or two in tonight. "I'm nervous, pumped, excited—all of the above," he says. Austin Britton-Davis looks tired. Garrett Sizemore took Tylenol PM last night. "I wanted to get some good sleep," he says. Sam Lukens went for a jog and "stared at the local cuisine." Mitchell Davis is "a little bored." Cameron Lane grades more papers. DeSantis takes the day off from running—he's slightly injured from the day before.

At 11:30, we cram equipment plus souvenirs into vans 19 and 21 and drive across the state.

JACKSONVILLE to LAKE CITY—There are no hotel rooms available in Gainesville because of some Gator Drag Race something or other, so we stay forty-five minutes north in Lake City. "You could get *one* hotel room in Gainesville," team mom Laura Topping says, "You just couldn't get *eleven* hotel rooms in Gainesville."

Players plop their bags down and run through their superstitious rituals, and then it's off to the field to take on Gainesville. Revenge is in order—after all, they run-ruled us here last year on this very trip.

Deal calls his troops over before the game.

"Let's not forget what happened last year," he says. "We got caught up in the facilities, we thought we were going to beat them, they beat us, and they disrespected us. Let's let last night be a blueprint—everybody's in the game from start to finish."

What followed was a long, wild, three-and-a-half-hour, seven-inning affair that saw HI pound out fourteen hits, use seven pitchers, and survive a cardiac bottom of the seventh inning to hold on for a 14–10 win.

When the dust cleared, freshman Sam Herrick picked up his first varsity victory, going three innings, fanning one, and giving up three runs. "It wasn't my best stuff, but I felt okay," he would say later.

At the plate, Jake Maziar went 4-for-4 with three singles, a double, and three runs scored. The catcher/first baseman is an incredible 8-for-12 on the trip so far. Skye Bolt went 2-for-4 with a three-run homer in the seventh. "I just relaxed finally and let my hands go," he said. Garrett Sizemore made the best of his appearance; he started in the outfield and went 2-for-5 with three RBIs. Mitchell Davis was 2-for-4 with two RBIs, and others who scratch out hits include Will Small, Howard Joe, Tal Kelsey, and Keller Latty.

An off-the-wall note: Howard Joe was hit by a pitch for the third straight game on this trip and the fourth game in a row. "It's in the same place every time," he says while rolling up his shirt. "Right there in the back." There's a welt proving him correct.

"Howard, why don't you just get out of the way!" a teammate yells.

Howard laughs, we board the bus, and we move on.

"We did a good job, particularly in running the bases tonight," Deal said back at the hotel. "We've done what we've come to do so far. Still, we're here to go 4–0 and to get better. Tomorrow's team is good, so we're going to have to stay sharp."

The kids order $242 worth of pizzas. And don't forget the breadsticks. This journalist is in bed, catching an interesting infomercial about staving off Alzheimer's. Unfortunately, he falls asleep before the author gives out the solution. Jesus weeps.

Quote of the day:
"I feel very close to all of these people. After all, I washed their underwear last night."
—Eva Murray (Skye's mom).

Saturday, March 10

Only the Buchholz Bobcats stand in the way of a perfect trip—a team reportedly fundamentally sound and capable of ending our five-game win streak. Though my wiring is down and I'm unable to switch you over to the HI website, please bear with me as I go into sportswriting mode:

GAINESVILLE—Holy Innocents' pitcher Daniel Topping was told his goal was to go at least four innings to give the tired pitching staff some rest. Needless to say, he was up for the challenge.

The junior threw a complete game, allowing two runs, fanning two, and walking nobody in an eighty-two-pitch effort in leading the Bears to a 5–2 win over Buchholz Saturday at Buchholz. With the win, Coach Dylan Deal's squad has now won six in a row and are 4–0 on their "spring training" Florida trip. They return home Monday to begin regional play with a 4:30 home date with Wesleyan.

"After I heard my goal was to go four, that made me want to go more," Topping said of his pitching goal. "My thoughts were to go all seven innings. I tried not to think of anything out there except going after the batters. My fastball was my main pitch; I struggled early with the curve, but I got it back as the game wore on."

"We got a great job out of Topping," Deal said. "Obviously, this was a great trip—we did enough to win. Still, we need to focus all seven innings—we didn't finish very well at the plate. On defense, I thought we might have been a little tired."

HI collected six hits on the day—Sam Jokerst was 2-for-3 and Howard Joe 2-for-4. Will Small and Sam Lukens also garnered hits.

The Bears scored two in the first, one in the third, and two in the fourth. In the opening frame, Lukens walked, took second on a wild pitch, and scored when Skye Bolt's sharp grounder was misplayed by the second baseman. Bolt scored on an RBI single by Joe.

In the third, Jake Maziar reached on an error before Joe and Jokerst both singled. Mitchell Davis then walked with the bases jammed to earn an RBI.

In the fourth, Small reached on an infield single, Lukens singled, and Bolt walked before Maziar delivered an RBI sacrifice fly. Lukens scored on a throwing error on a ball hit by Joe.

After the game, players, parents, and staff stand outside two buses in the Buchholz parking lot. Apparently a bird—let's call it a storm petrel with diarrhea—apparently entered bus 21's window while the game was going on and promptly—to use Waffle House terms—scattered, smothered, and covered every seat.

"That was a very thorough bird," Cefaratti and Olsen say as they wipe seat after seat. "I mean, what'd we ever do to him?"

Regardless, kids are successfully handed over to parents, bags are switched from van to car, golf clubs are rearranged, and two HI vans make the five-hour jaunt up I-75 back to Atlanta.

Closing Comments

It's Sunday as I write this; I'm going to switch over to Coach Deal in my brain, who spoke of the trip between games of spades on the bus last night. "I liked our mettle; I mean, we basically won four close games. Given that was four long days strung together; we could've easily taken a day off.

"I think D. Top taught the pitching staff a lesson Saturday: pound the zone, pitch to contact, and trust your defense. Each game had different heroes. It's great when you don't have to rely on just one guy.

"To be successful at baseball, you have to be courageous. You have to acknowledge—as a hitter, for example—that you're going to fail more than you're going to succeed, and you still put your best foot forward.

"I like the characters of this team. It was Sam Herrick giving it all he's got. It was Luke Wright coming on the trip and being our bullpen catcher. It was Alec Bicknese pitching and pinch running. There's more, but you get the point. You have to be vulnerable; you have to take care of each other. I respect all that."

The characters—I like that. In fact, I live for them. When school starts back, I'll always see the dirt on Luke's face after catching another round of bullpens. "I'm an All-Region bullpen catcher," he said with a laugh. I'll see Bicknese slamming down his glove and running a pole. I'll remember my own superstition— always putting my right hand on Deal's left shoulder when we prayed. I'll see Jim Voyles—who came on this trip despite being on the DL. "I'm frustrated, but I hope to be back. I' haven't been 100 percent in a year." Still, he was there!

I, too, could go on, but I close with this: At odd moments, I can still hear the ball pound off of Maziar's bat at Bolles. I can see him break into his home run trot before he spots Hoodie frantically motioning for him to sprint. I can see the panic on

Maziar's face as he breaks into his run. I can see the ball hitting the top of that fence, can see it strike the tree and bounce back into play. The umpire signals home run; the Bears' bench goes ballistic.

Or this one: The Bolles' guy singles up the middle, just out of the outstretched glove of Tal Kelsey. Skye Bolt lopes in, scoops it up with his glove, and fires a beeline arrow of a ball to Maziar, who is waiting at the plate. Maziar catches it, expertly drops his left knee down, and blocks the plate. The bench again goes ballistic before the ump even gives the signal that the Bolles' runner has officially been hosed.

Perhaps I'll always see these things. Still now, as I attempt to convert back into PR man/sub/tennis coach, this trip—perhaps the most successful in my years here—won't leave my head without a fight. It'll follow me down the halls, into classrooms; it will elbow me as I sleep. A card game, empty pizza boxes, batting practice, bunting runners over, cramming thirty-three smelly people onto two vans, nine guys fighting over two showers—yes, it is the characters. It's always the characters. I mean, what else is there?

Anyway, I'll blabber no more. I've put you through enough. Thanks for being with me; thanks for a great trip, and finally, thanks for being a character yourself.

Peace out.

Dunn Neugebauer
"Spring Training 2012"
March 6–10, 2012

Thanks for that report!

You're welcome, though I wish you'd help me with my golf game. It's so bad I was too embarrassed to play with the coaches.

As well you should be!

I just love getting abused by God!

You love it and you know it. Now, let's end this chapter with your true and funny story about golf. I know you're dying to tell it.

Okay, I'm golfing a few years ago with the cross country coach at Oglethorpe. We're on the first hole. He just sliced his drive—worse than I sliced mine—and he's in the woods, still about two hundred yards from the green. Bob—we'll call him Bob, since that is his name—pulls out his three iron.

Well, Bob swings with all his might—and misses the entire ball! With a confused look on his face, he glances over at me and says, "Man, this is a tough course!"

I laughed so hard I could hardly finish the hole!

And then?

Then we are on the fringe of the green, chipping up. Just to make conversation, I ask, "Where's the second hole?" Bob looks over at me and says, "You mean there's more!"

Nice. Glad you enjoyed spring break! And, as always, thank for the entertainment!

Always a pleasure, Your Honor; always a pleasure!

Two Months Later

Ahem!

God, it's me! I'm back!

Great! Welcome! You must've left me down in Jacksonville. Beautiful!

Sorry, I guess I've been ... busy.

With?

Well, school started back.

Of course! How dumb of me! I let you tell that silly little golf joke and then away you go!

Oops ... sorry.

Your loss, not mine. I've been busy with the economy, floods, a couple wars, a new presidential election coming up, and the 2012 Olympics. I've got plenty to do. Just think, if all these athletes pray to me during random regular-season games, imagine what's going to

happen to me during the Olympics! I'm going to have to hire some elves just to keep up with it all!

You could help me here—who should we vote for in the election?

You should perhaps decide whether you're a Democrat or a Republican first. You can't seem to get that straight.

I used to get all my political insights from my dad.

Dunn, I hate to be the bearer of bad news, but your father passed away fifteen years ago. No worries; we'll discuss you and your family later. Still … he would want you to move on.

Well, don't hold back on us—who's going to be the United States' next boss—Mitt Romney, Barack Obama, or someone else?

I'm thinking Jon Stewart right now, but I'm not really sure he'll be on the ballot.

Funny! Or maybe not. Still, you'll be happy to know I'm doing very well—I even think I've matured a little bit since our spring break trip.

Yes, you have. You've been doing great! Instead of watching reruns of *That '70s Show*, you've "graduated" to *NCIS* and *CSI Miami*. Nice upgrades! Bravo! Bravo!

You're mad, aren't you?

No, I told you—I'm busy! After I got thrown into and out of jail as a substitute teacher, my world has been—well—a whirlwind! Just trying to fix your economy is enough to make God want to resign! And don't get me started on your national debt! What do you people do with all that money? And don't worry, I'm not giving up on your

Braves yet, but those guys are just getting injured right and left! Do baseball players not condition themselves anymore? And why am I asking you? Am I not the one that's supposed to be God? Enough about me, though; I'm curious as to what's become of you in all this time we've been apart.

What do you want to know?

You tell me; I'm all ears!

Well, I've been pretty busy.

With what, with who ... your new girlfriend? Have you looked around your empty condo lately? You don't have a new girlfriend! Are you a bit confused?

So have you gotten arrested again lately?

No, have you? Though I'm proud of you for locking your car every now and then, your driving is another story. The fact that you haven't been pulled over since 2009 isn't saying much for your local police force! Enough about that; I'll play dumb here. Catch me up. Explain yourself.

Well, speaking of cars, somebody did break into mine the other day. Something about cars and me I guess.

And you locked your car?

I *did* lock it!

Yes, and you put your key on your front left tire. Brilliant! Whoever would think to look there? What runner doesn't put their keys on their car tires? How'd they ever crack that code?

Love the sarcasm—especially from God! What's that about?

I'm only learning from you, my friend, only learning from you. Continue with your life; I need a good chuckle.

Well, I'm still disguised as a public relations/sports information/ substitute teacher/car pool foreman/play-by-play announcer/scorebook keeper/tennis coach/cross-country coach down here in Atlanta. I would say I pretend to work and they pretend to pay me, but that's not accurate. I remember your hatred of complaining, so I'll say that my social life is going to get better, though they have etched my name on a bar stool at Teela Taqueria. Some of the patrons even call me Norm after the character in the old *Cheers* episodes.

Lovely, though I'm glad you remembered the complaining thing.

Spring tennis was drama-free—my number-one boy didn't kill anyone with his serve, and I didn't have to cut anybody. I still write sports for our website, and every now and then, someone actually reads some of my stuff!

I don't, but don't be offended.

I understand, particularly with the Olympics and the economy and all.

You're telling me what you've been doing, but to quote from the late Ernest Holmes, "How are you thinking?"

With my rear end, of course! Is there any other way?

At least you're honest. Why, just twenty minutes ago you told yourself you were, and I quote, "So dumb you didn't know if you were scratching your watch or winding your butt."

Oops, forgot about that.

Don't forget!

I try, but you get awful quiet sometimes.

If you'll pardon the awful pun, I'm anything but quiet. A smart aleck among you could even contend that I'm actually raising hell trying to reach you! I've been screaming at you for over a year!

How? Oh, never mind—it's those sign thingies again.

Still, don't beat yourself up. Take your anger out elsewhere—how about on the NBA? I mean, why do you guys have basketball season go on so long down there? It's May, and those tall guys are still hammering away at each other. Wasn't I clear when I made basketball a winter sport? What is it about winter that you people don't understand?

So you don't like basketball much?

I love it—in November, December, January, and February! And we'll even go into March, thanks to college hoops. But enough already! When it gets warm, break out the tennis rackets, the track shoes, the lacrosse sticks, the soccer balls, and the baseballs for my sake!

So you want to talk about sports?

No! I want to tell you I've missed you and all your wonderful tales about kissing pretty girls on their earlobes, liking John Denver and the Bee Gees, not being able to set your alarm on your fancy new iPhone, living your clueless social life, signing me up to be a teacher again, and then some! Where have you been? Things with me have been too serious! People don't talk to me unless things are serious! I'm

God, and I'm sick and tired of serious! Tell me a joke! Say something funny! Do something funny! Even think something funny!

Well, I did see something cute on Facebook again the other day.

Share it, please!

It read, "I want to live in a better world—a world where chickens can cross the road and not have their morals questioned!"

That's cute. I like that.

Oh, and I read another great quote the other day, but I don't want to get sued.

How can you get sued?

Because I don't know who said it. Also, can I get sued for writing about a conversation with you?

How? Why should anybody have a patent on who talks to me?

Well, there's this guy out in Oregon—

And he's a great guy! Forget lawsuits for a moment and tell me your quote. Then we'll go from there.

The quote reads, "Religion is for people who are afraid of hell. Spirituality is for people who have already been there."

You read that in one of Alan Cohen's books. Another great guy! And I suppose you can identify with that one. Let's get started, though. Have you been behaving yourself?

I am still yet to be convicted.

Beautiful! You are officially the Houdini of Sandy Springs, Georgia. Books should be written about you, movies crafted, songs written. And may the story of your life preempt all of your favorite television shows at least once! Herein sayeth the Good Lord!

Thanks, I think. And mentally I've been pretty positive, seriously!

Okay, now you're forcing my hand. Perhaps this is where we can begin. Let's take you as far back as … this morning. Your alarm clock went off; you yourself did not. You remained in bed for an extra nine minutes. Your first thought upon arising—and I realize some people will get offended at this language, but this was only what went on inside your head—was to call yourself a dumb ass.

Are we getting serious again?

Only for the last few remaining pages of this chapter. "Bear with me," as Peter Falk used to say on your heroic show. And don't say you're sorry, because you'll be being sorry for the wrong reasons. What if I told you that Bill Gates has overslept before? How about Steve Jobs? What about Donald Trump? Now, if I brought up those three men in a casual conversation, would you say, "Oh yeah, those guys are a bunch of dumb asses!"

I would think not.

At least we agree on something. In moving forward, while I'm offending people, let me make an amendment to one of your favorite rules while I'm at it.

You're going to change a rule? Don't go there. People have died for less.

I'm not going to mess it up or even question beliefs; I'm merely going to clarify one of your most popular rules.

Which one?

The Golden Rule.

The Golden Rule? Are you kidding me? That's the most widely quoted line, like, ever! Even I can quote the Golden Rule. Please tell me you're not going to mess with something as awesome as that? Why, I cracked on that rule when I was a kid, and my parents didn't let me play with my Lite-Brite or Tinker Toys, watch television, or write in my diary for two weeks!

You played with Lite-Brites and Tinker Toys, *and* you wrote in a diary when you were a kid?

Sure.

You got beaten up a lot, didn't you?

Well …

Relax! I'm kidding. You've got to start getting used to a God that has a sense of humor. You use yours; why can't I use mine?

That makes sense, though many people will never see it that way.

And that saddens me greatly. And, as people tell you all the time with your job, you can quote me on that! Now let's get back to the Golden Rule. Start by reciting it to me.

That's easy: "Do unto others as you would have them do unto you." That's the most straightforward, honest philosophy-of-life quotation ever. Please don't undo all my years of thinking in one fell swoop.

We just briefly discussed your "years of thinking," but let's stay with the rule. Are you ready?

No, not at all. I don't want to have my feeble mind blown over something so awesome and filled with common sense.

Please, just hear me out.

Okay, go ahead.

Okay, the "Do unto others" part is great. People pretend to understand it, they pretend they live by it, they recite it, and, for the most part, they say they know it. It's the "as you would have them do unto you" part I'm amending.

Why?

Because you all do "unto you" so poorly! You're nicer to strangers than you are to yourselves, for heaven's sake! You treat your rabid zombie ferrets better—though they do deserve the very best, and pets are one of my greatest inventions—except for the infamous cockroaches, but still.

Don't get me started on cockroaches, but okay, okay, I got it!

Actually you don't, but in moving forward, let's just say it like this: do unto others after you have first and foremost learned how to properly do unto yourself! Quote and end quote. Make it a Golden Rule, subset A if you have to, but do *not* forget it. And please, for God's sake—and I mean that literally—learn it.

I just read that sentence, and it sounds a little bit selfish. First and foremost learning how to properly do unto yourself.

That's because your mind just completely—and I mean completely—went into the gutter. If you go there, you're going to have to change the title of this thing to *Perverted Conversations with God*, and you're liable to get shot at your local bookstore. But seriously, somewhere inside that granite head of yours, I know you are getting this.

Wow, this is kind of blowing me away! I would've never thought in a million years that of all the things, that's the thing you would attack.

I'm not attacking it; I'm merely getting you to—like Wayne Dyer says—change your definition of who you are, hence how you should treat yourself. In your case, for example, you treat yourself like a dumb ass. Again, I'm only quoting you. Or in some cases, like a buffoon. Now, are you supposed to go out and treat others like a dumb ass or a buffoon? Seriously? I mean, that's the way you treat yourself, so are others supposed to treat you that way?

God, I hope not.

God does hope not—thanks for putting those correct words into my mouth. They are supposed to treat you the way you are supposed to treat you—as a human with a God inside of you, a God waiting to be a companion and a cocreator; a God that doesn't need to be forgotten for months; a God who is pricelessly planning the upcoming games of the Olympiad; a God who invented liquid soap, the shoehorn, and Raid bug spray; a God who had nothing to do with the invention of the designated hitter—that was you humans' fault again—a God who listens, cares, and, most importantly, loves. Now, did you get that, you dumb ass buffoon?

Are you really calling me that?

No, *never*, but you are! Now stop it! Quit doing that. Say something funny instead—sublimate! Next time you oversleep, if that is such an offensive thing, just realize how human you are. As I said, some very intelligent people on your planet have overslept before. And, believe it or not, Rafael Nadal and Roger Federer have double faulted before. And Steve Jobs missed a turn—more than once. And Albert Einstein forgot to do something—more than twice. And as I said, I made a mistake when I invented the cockroach! Please tell me you're getting my point!

How could I not; you're pounding it into my very soul. Though I know of a lot of people who will have trouble forgiving you about this cockroach thing. (More on this later.)

I'm a God who can only say he's sorry. And as for me pounding this into your soul, that is good! That's exactly where I want it pounded—into your pizza-eating, mosquito-infested, Teela Taqueria–drinking, late-sleeping, southern-boy soul.

That kind of just rearranged my entire brain—for what that's worth.

That's worth a lot; that's the whole point. But don't blame me for what goes on inside that brain of yours! Unless thinking is being seriously changed, things will continue to be seriously damaged—like your planet, for example. So go spread my amendment, if you would. Dare to be insulted for having the nerve. Be prepared to get called a name or three. But get it out there; the sooner the better. Are you getting this?

I think so, though you never know with me.

Well, let's change the subject—lighten things up, if you will. What did you do this weekend?

Why does God have to ask me what I did this weekend? I mean, don't you know?

I'm happy to say I do, because I was there—thanks to your finally remembering to ask after a few months. But I'm trying to make a point or two here. Now, tell both of your readers and me what you did this weekend.

I went to our school's baccalaureate Friday night and graduation Saturday morning. That was the highlight. I mean, you don't want to know the rest of it.

I do know, but let's start with the baccalaureate and then move on to graduation. Tell me what you heard Friday night in the bishop's speech.

I slept through most of it.

Sadly you did, but you "just happened" to wake up at a key and coincidental time. Tell us what you liked about the speech.

Oh, that's easy—the part about the bumper sticker.

Please share that with us.

The speaker talked about a bumper sticker he saw that read, "Be yourself. Everyone else is taken."

Oh, clever. Actually it was Oscar Wilde who said that. Excellent advice for people about to go off to college, don't you think— particularly with the peer pressure of that age. High school and college are really tough years as far as peer pressure.

Agreed!

But I'm not letting you off that easily. Let's move on to graduation. No, let me be more specific: You're driving away from graduation to get your car fixed. Tell us what you're thinking about.

I'd be uncomfortable with that. Also, I was unhappy because I had to get my car fixed in the first place!

First of all, your car has been more than good to you. Why not appreciate it? As for your thoughts, don't you think I know them?

It's not that, but it's just that my thoughts were ... almost on the arrogant side. I don't want to be arrogant. Being arrogant can get you beaten up faster than playing with Tinker Toys and writing in diaries. I learned that the hard way.

I am not going to let you steer me away from this; please remember who you're arguing with! I would say that your thoughts were spot on. Now please share them, and we'll let both the readers decide. Tell us your thoughts.

Well, I was going through the last few years in my head since I moved from South Florida back to Atlanta. I was thinking of my times at my school and how fortunate I've been. I was thinking of how I love my job, how lucky I've gotten, and how, well, almost successful I've been.

Keep going. You're dancing around the point and you know it. Now *why* have you been "lucky" and successful?

I think it's because of my love for the school, my love for what I do, and my desire to get up in the morning and get to work. I mean, you always do well doing what you love.

That's true for the most part, but keep going. Tell us your own "bumper sticker," if you will.

I thought you wanted to lighten up?

I changed my mind. God can change his mind, can't he?

I would think so.

Well, go ahead; tell us how you summed it up. I'll help you—the writer in you always wants to try to express things up in a sentence or so. You're driving down Mt. Vernon Highway and you're trying to sum up your happiness and your success at your school in one sentence. I would say you succeeded. Now please tell us the sentence.

The sentence that popped into my head was, "If you lead with love, all else will follow."

Hmm, you thought of that?

No, I'm going to give you credit and say that *you* put that into my head.

And I'm going to give it right back to you, because *you* allowed me in there. You were with me, you were thinking of me; you were thinking of peaceful thoughts, love, all of the above. You let me in, hence your "coincidental" thought. Now, repeat that.

Repeat what?

Repeat that sentence. Besides, we have to end this chapter. We need a break. Plus, a second baseman just homered down in Miami. He's summoning me. He should be; second basemen rarely hit homers. Now end the chapter with that sentence.

Okay. If you lead with love, all else will follow.

Thank you.

No, thank you!

Meditation, Blogs, Ticks, and Zits

Hey, God, it's my birthday!

So what? Quit celebrating; you were an accident!

So that explains it!

Explains what?

Why I'm bumbling around down here. I wasn't even supposed to hatch! Why did you do that to me?

Just kidding! Have a blessed and loving day. What are your plans?

After looking over my agenda carefully, I have come to realize I don't have one.

Boo! What a cop-out! You're living in a city with millions of people—including eight snow trucks, by the way—and you're telling me you have nothing to do!

What do snow trucks have to do with anything? It's eighty-five degrees out.

Nothing, I was just being cute. Now go ahead with your day.

I have my tennis coaching evaluation at nine thirty; I get a free coffee at Starbucks thanks to some of our students, I have a softball game at six thirty, and then afterward—well, perhaps I shouldn't tell you what I'm going to do.

You're going to do your imitation of Norm at your local watering hole!

Right! I guess it's pointless to try to keep stuff from God, huh?

Pointless times twelve, you might say. Why don't you count your blessings today? With this being your big day and all, why don't you live it right for a change?

I've read about doing that; I've just never done it. Where would I start?

Let's see … you went hiking with your friend Jolene the other day, and you only got two ticks on you; that's something to be grateful for. You pulled them both off without further ado or diseases. Trust me; that could've been bad.

Is that what I want to be grateful for, a lack of ticks? And speaking of which, what did you invent those things for?

Perhaps there was a purpose, perhaps I mixed my chemicals wrong again—not important for now. How about your health? You just had your physical, right? And you got a good report?

And boy did he look thoroughly!

Quit complaining! Do you want twenty seconds of pain or embarrassment, or do you want prostate cancer? Complaining— there's an idea—we're going to start with that.

What about complaining?

You're not going to do it—all day! Period!

Want to bet? What if *Family Guy* is a repeat? What if I can't get a good parking spot when I go run at the river? What if there's a long line at Trader Joe's? What if there's a ridiculously long line at The Dollar Tree—

Stop! Just because you're joking doesn't mean you're not complaining! You've always hid behind your humor, unfortunately with a lot of success.

But I can't fool you!

You got it!

So how am I going to pull this off?

You will, and you will like it. Today is a gratitude-filled, no-complaining, Dunn-bites-his-lip-about-85-percent-of-the-time type of day.

Wow, this will be the quietest birthday I've ever spent.

Sadly, you're probably right. So let's start. Where are you right now?

I'm at work—even though I don't have to be. I'm only a ten-month employee—the beauty of education!

See, can't you be grateful for that? You could actually go home today and set your alarm clock for a month from now, and all would be fine. You have nowhere to be, no one to see, no deadlines, nothing.

That's not always a good thing, though. People need companions! Where's mine? My condo is often way too quiet!

Was that a complaint?

No, just a question. I don't feel we were meant to roam this earth alone.

And you feel you are alone?

Yes, even though all of my readings tell me otherwise! I mean, I'm over my wife, but I miss the companionship—somebody to go hiking or to a brunch or a movie or rafting or walking with, or someone to complain about me when I burp at the dinner table.

Among other things, but I think I got it. And you feel these people don't exist?

They exist, but where in the h … I mean, where are they?

Be happy with what you've got—genuinely happy—and it will grow. Let's just say your lack of gratitude equals your lack of a social life.

Could you explain that?

You're focusing on what you don't have—a companion. You're focused on loneliness and boredom. When you focus on that, guess what?

You get more of that!

You got it! Now go ahead. You were saying …

I spent my first day of summer yesterday watching *Walker, Texas Ranger*! I hate *Walker, Texas Ranger*! I mean, no offense to Chuck Norris or anything, but get real!

Have you ever tried, I don't know, going somewhere? Doing something? Calling a friend? And if you tell me you don't have any friends, I'll zap you so fast you'll feel like you're on Broil in your microwave! Here's the irony: you're sitting around waiting on me, and I'm over here sitting around waiting on you. It's the same way with you writing this book—I'm waiting on you to start; you're waiting on me to zap an idea into your head. Haven't you heard the saying, "When a web is begun, God sends thread"?

Great saying! I'll write that one down. But back to the point, I am doing something today!

That's right, you're getting some work done. The angels rejoice, and I'm conducting the choir. Now enjoy your fifty-second birthday, for God's sake!

I didn't want people to know how old I am.

Why not? It's a landmark day. After all, all four of your personalities are thirteen years old! They are all certified teenagers! And most of them are good personalities. I'll grade you at three out of four—75 percent. That's probably the best grade you've made in a long time!

Thanks, I think.

Now don't just tell me about your day; tell me about your thought processes while you go about it. What are you thinking, what are you thinking, what are you thinking?

Okay, I'm going to try this. I just had my tennis evaluation, and it went well.

What, she didn't fire you? Good grief, who in the world is your athletic director?

What?

Just kidding. Go ahead. Tell me your successes instead of your screw-ups. And by the way, quit being so hard on yourself. Your screw-ups sometimes make my day; they give me something to laugh about. Now continue. Your day is starting great; one of your many bosses had nice things to say about you. Maybe you could build on that instead of poking holes in it? Just a thought. Speaking of thoughts, you had a good one while you were in your meeting. Please share.

I just made myself a mental note to stay busy this summer—to travel, keep jogging, reach out to people, write more, and basically resist the lures of my wonderful couch, which has a really bad habit of making me lie down on it too many times during the summer months.

Aren't you going back to running camp again?

You know the answer to that—of course I am. You want to go with me?

No!

Just no? You don't want to … maybe reconsider … thinking about it some more?

No! What in the world do you do at a running camp—besides run?

You're telling me God doesn't know what goes on at a running camp? That's all the more reason you should go up with me!

Of course I know what goes on; I'm just busting your chops.

So come join me! Didn't you have fun in Jacksonville?

Jacksonville was fine, but I'm not going to running camp with you.

Why?

I don't have any running shoes.

God doesn't own a pair of running shoes? I've probably got some extra lying around the house. What size shoe do you wear?

My foot is adaptable.

Of course it is; why am I not surprised! Still, I think you'd love running camp.

"Running" and "camp"—I'm not sure those two words ever belong in the same sentence!

This sounds like God is a non-runner. Do you not like sports?

I invented sports. Now let's move on. Perhaps I'll join you at camp, particularly when you're doing speed work. That's usually when you call my name.

I don't do speed work anymore.

With the size of the copperheads I'm going to put on your trail, brother, you will! You can trust me on that one!

Great, something to look forward to besides running up and down mountains! Can't wait!

Let's move on from running camp—I'll join you when you least expect it. Still, you're once again dancing around what I wanted you to share with both of your readers. Go ahead, out with it!

What are you asking me for? I forgot already.

You had a very good thought this morning at your meeting, and I want you to share it, granite head! Don't waste a perfectly good thought when I send it to you. Repeat it! Remember it! Live it!

Okay. It was just a "use-it-or-lose-it" type thing. The thought was, "If you don't play your cards, God will shuffle your deck."

Wow, you're on a roll. Perhaps you should write that one down next to the one about the thread. Hey, I have a crazy idea, Mr. Writer: why not write a lot of these down where you can refer to them when your head gets stuck in ... well, you know?

Okay, I have now officially written it down.

Sorry to keep interrupting. Now continue please. I want to hear more from the mental framework and less from the physical.

(We pause here momentarily while the writer goes off to a quiet place to conduct himself a little experiment. You can decide how things went.)

Okay, I followed your orders a while ago.

Scratch that! I never "order" you to do anything.

Sorry. I carried forward with my homework for today—you know, the gratitude, no-complaining, bite-my-lip, try-to-think-of-more-bumper-stickers type thing.

And?

So I go sit in an unoccupied room at work. It's summer, so not many people are around. Speaking of which, that's a little on the depressing side right there—walking down the hallways of an empty high school.

Please share; why is that so depressing? In fact, don't just share, but also tell us what you wrote about the hallways so non-teachers can understand.

You want me to put that in here?

Yes, I gave you the idea. For once, you actually acted on it. Go ahead.

Okay, here goes:

The Sounds of Summer

When high school is in session, a casual walk down any hallway is the definition of adrenaline. The kids come at you at 150 miles per hour, with gusts up to 250, with their tales, woes, injuries, test grades, love lives or lack thereof—all that and then some. In fact, being an employee at a local high school, I will often walk out among the halls when I hear the bells ring, my goal being to pick up on their energy. Trust me, if you need a pick-me-up, it's way better than vanilla coffee with cream and teeth-rotting amounts of sugar.

Now, however, that same walk is a different thing; more of a downer, if you will. Lockers sit empty, idle. None are opening and closing, and more importantly, none are slamming with authority. The bells are turned off. There is no chatter, no trash on the floors, no signs on each locker, no happy birthday wishes pasted on locker 134, no "Go Bears" on the one right above it. No, instead there is—in a word—nothing.

Today I could actually hear my feet strike the floor. For that matter, I could hear myself breathing. From August through May, you can't even hear yourself think. You can't walk two steps without seeing someone, picking up on a conversation, finishing another, well-wishing someone, or cheering up someone else. In short, when the bells are set to do their cosmic duty every fifty minutes, each step is another adventure; it's always (one word and two) a case of sensory overload times twelve.

Except in June and July. I heard no bells ringing, but I walked the halls anyway. I saw nothing, heard nothing, felt out of place.

In summary, sometimes silence is the loudest sound there is.

Peace out!

There, that's from my blog.

Well said, but don't get cocky; nobody ever reads your blog.

I don't know if you're serious or not, but it doesn't matter. As you always say, let's move on!

We will. I want to focus on one of your last lines: "Sometimes silence is the loudest sound there is." You also learned that from living in an empty condo down in Florida after your divorce. I meant to tell you that all you had to do was turn on the TV, but I didn't want to interrupt you when you were on such a negative roll.

Why not?

Kidding again? Boy, for someone with a sense of humor, sometimes you really don't have a sense of humor! But let's get back to your "experiment."

Okay, it's an empty office, the lights are out, and there's a computer chair I sit in right up against the wall. In fact, if you lean back, you can fall asleep. In fact—

Okay, we get it. The chair is comfortable. Continue please.

I'm sitting there, eyes all closed, feet on the floor, hair all combed, not a tick on my body to be found. But if there is another tick, could you please let me know? I don't want to get Lyme disease and—

Ahem.

Sorry, I can't help it. I start breathing very slowly, very deeply. From what I've read, that helps a lot.

Of course it does. We've already discussed the "count to ten" and "deep breathing" thing earlier.

I remember.

Sorry to interrupt. Please continue.

I'm breathing in to the count of four, breathing out to the count of four. Why four? I don't know. Why not? Maybe it's because of that old Spearmint gum commercial.

No, that was "Three, three, three mints in one!" I might have botched some chemicals when I made your memory! But let's move on—four is fine. After all, there are four sides to a square, four bases in baseball, four on the floor—

Okay, ahem yourself. I'm picturing sunlight over water; that always has seemed peaceful to me. I'm sitting comfortably, my good shirt on, my teeth brushed and everything, gazing out into this water—which is ripple free, I might add.

Unlike your mind, as I'm sure we will see, but go ahead.

So I start chanting in my mind, really softly. I mean, if I do it out loud, the maintenance people might make a few phone calls and have me committed.

They should join you, but go ahead.

Well, if you can get arrested as a substitute teacher—being who you are and everything—please imagine what could happen to little old me. And they wouldn't let me out, either. I wouldn't last a day in prison!

Please continue with your attempts at meditation and try to stop getting off track. Did you quit taking your ADD medicine?

I thought about it this morning; then I forgot.

That's funny ... actually not so funny.

So I'm humming along, picturing my little water and my sunlight, and I've got this "Om" thing going in my little head. I'm thanking God for this, and I'm thanking God for that.

Could you be more specific here and quit being vague? What goes on in your mind is important!

That's what you think! Well, never mind. I'm thanking God for this day, the bed I woke up in, the car I drove to work in, the healthy legs I ran with, and my colleagues. Things are feeling great.

And?

And then I shuddered, because I figured *Ain't No Sunshine* had to be playing somewhere. I mean, that's what happens, right?

Ahem.

Sorry. I'll continue. I have this warm and fuzzy feeling in my gut; I even have a couple of chill bumps working up and down my spine. I'm thanking God, chanting, sitting up straight and wide-awake, and then I think, *Man! I've got a dentist appointment next month. Lord, I hope my new insurance works. My plan at the other place blows! Oops, sorry, God!* I then return myself to giving thanks. *Thank you for my family, thank you for all the people who have wished me a happy birthday, thank you for … Man, that girl at the river this morning was* hot! *I wonder if she's taken. Oh, the things I'd … Oops, sorry again, God. Thank you for my comfortable work environment, thank you for the air we breathe. Thank you again for my health; we always tend to take that for granted … What in the world is wrong with the Braves? They've lost eight of their last nine! Are they tired? Are they old? Are they just not that good? Oops, sorry again. Thank you for the stars, thank you for the pets … Man I miss Jasper! Whatever happened to that dog? Should I get a dog? I mean, I don't have a great place to walk one, but speaking of companionship, wasn't I just complaining about a lack of companionship … Yeah … a dog … Oops, sorry again. Thank you for letting me be bounced-check free for the second year in a row. Thank you for … I wonder where they're taking me for my birthday tonight? I don't want to go to Meehan's again! I'm only in love with two of their bartenders, and besides … And another thing, why is it that I'm over fifty years old and I'm still getting zits? What's up with that? I mean, how old do you have to be before you outgrow the things? Or do you ever?*

I could go on, but do you get the point?

I do. And I contend that I'm proud of you.

How? There are a bunch of wild squirrels running around inside my head 24-7! My mind changes literally within the blinking of an eye. It's *frustrating*! I'm sure meditation is *great* for you; I totally believe it. But I read all these books that say "Change your thoughts, think positive, don't think negative," and I'm like, *really?* Is it that $#$# easy? I might as well run a marathon, pick up dinner, head home, and build a house or two before sundown. Just how in the world are we supposed to do all this stuff?

I love it when you get frustrated!

Thanks a lot!

No, seriously. It means you care; you're on the right track. And I'm going to repeat myself: I'm proud of you, first of all. Second of all, keep doing that.

Keep doing what, complaining?

No, stop doing that. Keep attempting to meditate! And stop being so hard on yourself! You are a human; you will screw up often. Learn from it. Write it down. And keep doing what you did this morning.

What did it accomplish?

Well, how about the idea of getting a dog? Is that a bad idea? The odds are you won't love him as much as you did Jasper, but dogs make great companions. And how awesome was Jasper! To think I actually invented a dog that can't bark—a Basenji. Who but me could've thought of that one?

It almost sounds cruel. How could you have a dog that can't bark? Are there any cats that can't meow? Are there any of us rednecks who have never had a Budweiser?

Nope, not going to work. I'm going to make you stay with this meditation conversation. After all, you will get better at it as you

practice. **Quit trying to hit a home run your first time! Did you try to run a marathon your first time out?**

No, I only ran one mile on the track. I got so tired I had Tourette's syndrome the last two laps.

Yes, you offended a devout Christian, if I'm not mistaken.

I did; I'm afraid I scared that poor man … and he didn't even let me apologize. He just ran away. It was so bad I felt offended myself, but go ahead.

No, you go ahead. Set a goal for one minute—just one minute to not think about dentists, hot women, the Braves, zits, and all the other assorted crap that flies in and out of that skull of yours. I promise you some good stuff will work its way in there. I promise! You just have to work at it.

I'll try it.

I've heard this before. You were going to try keeping me around as your companion, and then you disappeared over and again. You were going to start locking your car, and you got robbed again.

You're still not going to tell me who did it, are you?

No, listen! Well, let's try it this way, because I know you won't. Do you have any clue how much better shape the world would be in if they would start and/or finish each day by "going to God," as you like to say?

You mean I have to lock myself in an empty classroom and ask you if there are any more ticks on me? Couldn't you just tell me? Also, what's the true story about zits? Why do we even get those things in high school—

especially right in time for the prom! And let's not even talk about the prom; that's another book right there! And would meditation help the Braves? Man, when runners are on base, they can't hit their butts with both hands! You're saying with the Olympics, elections, wars, floods, famines, and the like, our best bet is to sit in an empty room and meditate?

Stop it! If I were in human form, I'd probably cuff you a time or two. It frustrates me that you're so close but you can't—or won't—close the deal.

What deal?

The deal that is your mind. It's both the best thing and the worst thing that you've got going. You have to train it! You have to work at it. By the time the alarm clock goes off every morning, you're already calling yourself names and griping about your agenda (or lack thereof), wondering if you're going to be able to throw strikes on the mound in your softball game, wondering why you haven't met "the one" yet, wondering if there will be a line at the Dunkin' Donuts drive-through. Never once do you stop—or even attempt to stop—and think of and thank me. It's not that I need it; it's more that you do! Lord, I could help you people!

This could get frustrating.

Did you say "could"? Just kidding. I'm tired of being serious again, so I'm going to leave you now and let you get back to it.

Get back to what, meditating?

No, get back to work! Your boss is coming.

The Voices of Summer

So, God, what do you want to do today? Head to St. Simons to see a friend? Go to Statesboro to visit my brother? Back to school to do some work? Suggestions? Buehler? Buehler?

How about laundry? Have you looked in your laundry hamper lately? I think things are starting to infest it. And how about getting rid of your clutter—in your house, in your car, and in your office? Have you ever heard the saying, "Cluttered house, cluttered mind"?

How could you possibly say my mind is cluttered?

Ahem!

Sorry, somehow I knew I wasn't going to get away with that one.

Let me put it this way: What if you did meet a nice woman—a potential companion? What would she say if she came over and saw where you live, for me's sake. I mean, she could wander into your bathroom and never be seen again! There's another saying: "If you met the perfect one, would she date you?"

That's clever. Never thought of that.

Well, think of it. You have to prepare for and believe in the things you're looking for. As the saying goes, "Change your feelings, change your destiny." So your summer project—besides doing this writing and besides getting me back on the substitute teacher list—

Ahem yourself.

You're right. I knew I couldn't get away with that one. You're going to clean at least two layers of grime out of your shower, you're going to throw away all that crap you haven't looked at in your closet, you're going to give away the clothes you don't wear anymore and maybe some of the ones you do. You're going to—

But I like my stuff.

I hate to say this, but when did you move from South Florida back to Atlanta?

May 30, 2007—it was my forty-seventh birthday.

And yesterday you just had your fifty-second birthday. Now, how many times have you opened up your closet, gone through those boxes, and looked at the stuff that is in there?

That's an easy one—zero!

There's another saying: "Put your stuff in a box, store the box somewhere, and if you haven't looked at it a year later, throw it away! You don't need it! Obviously your life is moving along without it!"

What about the memories?

What about making new ones? At least clean out the boxes! I guarantee it; you could condense six of those boxes down into one.

Having one box in the closet isn't bad. Haven't six that are unlooked at is. And why is your closet full of clothes? You wear the same thing practically every day!

There's a Goodwill right down the street.

So use it! You could even get a tax write-off for it.

Don't get me started on taxes!

You're right; look who I'm talking to. Now, you showered this morning, right?

Where are you going with this? I am a clean person, if nothing else.

Well, while both your feet were getting stuck to the grime-infested floor, did you remember me?

Well … no. I forgot. I'm sorry. Actually, I didn't forget!

You're right—you cussed me when you almost slipped. Luckily, the filth kept both of your feet glued to the floor. Still, I'm not chastising you; I'm just bringing up a point. Now, let's get back to your summer. How did your birthday dinner go?

Great! I practically fell in love!

Not so great! She'll be engaged by Monday! You sure know how to pick them, I tell you. Let me help you here: the idea is to fall in love with the *single* women, not the ones who are excited about their future with their husband-to-be.

Couldn't I apply for the job?

You could have—over three years ago in this case.

But I didn't know her over three years ago!

Whose fault was that? She worked a building near you. Of course, you didn't know this, because your head was inserted somewhere else at the time. Still, I'm not going to rip into you for that. You've made progress! You're no longer sucking down antidepressants! You're no longer feeling sorry for yourself! You're taking action! You're doing things!

This is true, for the most part.

Anyway, she's a great girl—awfully attractive, just your type. But … no. Ding, thanks for playing! You'll find a great girl. This one is a great girl, but she's not *your* great girl. Dream all you want, but move on! Your future is waiting.

Does my future include bad reruns?

You tell me, does it?

Well, while I'm on this grateful kick: I would like to thank you for sending the girl in question down here. She's sweet and fun to look at, and she added an exclamation point to my birthday—which was a good day anyway.

Thanks! Now quit begging. She's taken. Move on.

Okay, back to summer.

Tell both of your readers about the trip you and Phil are planning.

Well, the idea is to fly west—out to Seattle—and then jump on Amtrak and cruise over to Portland. Hey, I could even say hello to my ex-wife when I'm out in Seattle! Boy, won't she and her new husband be so happy to see me! What do you think?

Perhaps not, but great idea on the trip! Do you know how many people would kill to have the opportunity to do that? Why are you even hesitating?

Well, there are the finances, and there's the matter of getting up and actually doing it.

You're killing me here! Remember one of your favorite sitcoms, *That '70s Show*?

Of course I remember! I still watch it—they show reruns of it on cable. In fact, just the other night they had the one on where—

Stop! The reason I bring it up is this: if I were in human form, I would become Red Forman and I would stick my foot so far—

Wow! This sounds so vulgar coming from God!

Well, how in the world am I supposed to get your attention! The sacred, ritualistic form doesn't work with you! In fact, it doesn't work with a lot of people—a whole slew of them. Now, back to your trip, Phil is flying back to Atlanta in a month. He's doing fine, by the way—a good human, that Phil. Both of you: Get out of town! Go! Meet people—yes, even in the places you hang out at. Talk to a farmer, fall in love with a waitress in a random diner, hang out in a local coffee shop, go for a jog and get lost, go for a hike and wade in a creek, stay at least one night in a hotel you probably can't afford, meet a stranger on a train, take in a concert whether you like the performer or not, go to a comedy club, take a tour of some random town. Wow, the potential

here is endless. And, not to throw some more pressure on you, but you could—gasp—write about it. And I want to go!

You mean I have to invite you before you can go? But wait, you've got the election coming up and the Olympics, wars, bar mitzvahs, people scoring touchdowns, second basemen hitting home runs, women in labor, beggars on Roswell Road, out-of-work actors—

Stop! I'll go with you regardless, but will *you* take me with you? Or will I just be off in the background somewhere, laughing at the silly choices you make in life? I'm not going to beg—hint, hint—but I would love to take that trip.

Cool! Where do you want to go? Want to catch a Mariners game? Probably not as neat a stadium as Wrigley or Fenway, but still—I haven't watched an American League game in forever!

Ahem.

Sorry, I have this smart aleck side about me.

Really? No kidding! How about going places you haven't been? Remember the line from Neale Donald Walsch: "Life begins at the end of your comfort zone." Remember *your* line about the comfort zone?

You people have a line for everything!

So what did you expect!

But I like my comfort zone!

You should; you've built a fine one. Congratulations already! Now get the hell out of it!

Good Lord!

Exactly, and thank you! That's exactly what I'm trying to be here—a good Lord! And read the line again—get the *hell* out of it! Now, back to your travels: You've rarely been out west. You've never seen Colorado or Oregon. I did some of my finest work when I made some of those states. You yourself have seen the Grand Canyon and Hoover Dam. Try some other places—the Grand Tetons or the hills of Montana. I think you will like what I've done, for the most part. In fact, many who wander out to Colorado never come back!

That's what I'm afraid of.

You of all people shouldn't be afraid. I can't even get you off of your couch. Do I have to give you the Red Forman reminder again?

No! I get it. We really are supposed to go on some type of trip.

And you really should! And as I've said, I would *love* to go with you. And if you don't go on this trip, and if you even consider blaming me—

I'm not going to blame you. Why would I do that?

Oh, you'd be surprised at the blame I take sometimes. Again, people are down there waiting on me. I'm up here, over there, and all around, waiting on them. It's an endless cycle some never escape. They're born, they live, and they die, all the while still waiting. Do you remember your friend Craig Milam?

How could I forget Craig Milam? He called the other day and—

Quiet! Let me make my point. Do you remember what he would say to you when you two got bored in college?

Yes, he used to say, "We need to do something, even if it's wrong!"

Glad you remember.

You want me to go do something wrong?

No, but I want you to listen to the philosophy! You're a morally good person—I know you're not going to rob someone at gunpoint, rape and pillage a village, and shoot up a bank and take bags of money. It's not you—and you're welcome for that. But listen to Craig's words and the feeling behind them.

It worked in college.

For the most part, it did. There is an exception or two in there, but we won't go into that, or this book might get too long. Still, congrats to you and Phil on this trip. See what I'm doing? I'm congratulating you in advance.

Ah, cute!

Thanks! Now have fun. When do we leave?

What about money?

What about it?

I'm worried about the cost!

Do you believe in the law of attraction?

Yes, I was attracted last night.

Forget last night! Now, back to the law of attraction, and this brings up a very good subject we've already talked about—money. I only bring it up again because it always comes up again and again. It probably will continue to come up, but let's review.

I have no problem with money today. In fact, I checked my balance this morning, and my micro-deposit went through!

Yes, you did check your balance, and I'm *really* glad you said that.

Said what?

What in the world is a micro-deposit?

Oops, I slipped up again. I was supposed to change the newscast to say, Dunn's wonderful, gratitude-filled, pleasingly loving, helpful, assisting currency has just plopped itself into his gargantuan, truckload of a bank account. In fact, bank managers and loan officers are still scratching their heads over what occurred just this morning at approximately 3:34 a.m. Dunn Is Rich Eastern Standard Time—

Enough, smart guy, though I'm glad you caught yourself for a change.

I'll catch on sooner or later. It's just probably going to be later in my case—a whole lot later. Still, getting paid is good, yes?

It is what it is. Still, I'm glad you're catching on. See? Your first and initial thought was a complaint!

How do I fix that? As you say, I can be somewhat of a granite head when it comes to matters such as these. Matters such as ... you know ... life itself.

You change it by changing it—nothing more, nothing less. Now take your trip, or you will be flogged! I want you to see Seattle—and no, not your ex-wife! Phil wants to go to Portland. Don't waste three hours at a baseball game—you can do that here—plus the game's going to be a rout anyway. (Quick, call Las Vegas!) Tell your Sandy Springs Dunkin' Donuts good-bye for about ten days; I'll tell them not to call the cops or alert the media. Say good-bye to runs at the river for a while.

I think I really am going to go on this trip. Earlier I was just talking it up, seeing how you would react.

Quit trying to frustrate me!

But I love it when God gets frustrated!

Shouldn't you be a little nervous about that? Don't you remember what the bullies on the playground would say to you before they rearranged your face? "You better watch who you're messing with, boy!"

So are you telling me you were actually with me when I was getting realigned on the playground when I was a kid? And you didn't stop them? I could've used a little help, you know.

Oh, you could've used a *lot* of help, but let's not change the subject! Fly west, young man, fly west. Split the cost, stay in a hostel, camp out in the mountains, swim with the ducks, order something besides vanilla coffee, and get out and stay out of your comfort zone. You can do this!

Go ye forth to grand adventures!

You've got it! This shouldn't be so hard. This should be—as you people like to say—a no-brainer. Now have fun! And you're welcome!

I'm ready! Let's go.

Don't get ahead of yourself. Phil doesn't fly in until early next month.

Sorry.

Don't be. I like your spirit. Now keep it! And by the way—it's almost three o'clock. You forgot to eat!

The History of the 5K

Are you avoiding me again?

No, it's June already; we started our cross country training today. I'm simply writing up the history of the 5K for my kids. Want to hear it?

You know the history of the 5K?

Of course. Want to hear it?

Why? Am I going to regret this if I say yes?

You probably will, but here goes:

Circa 1676 BC—before the computer chip, stopwatches, electric razors, eight-track tape players, and *Columbo* episodes—a group of cave people got really, really bored. Besides being bored, this clan was also incredibly dumb, so much so that God wouldn't even give them an Old Testament mention when he inspired smarter people to write the Bible years later.

May I interrupt?

Of course, you're God. You can pretty much do whatever you want to, I would imagine.

What is it with you and Columbo?

He acted dumb, but he was smart. I like that. Plus, as a kid, I used to watch the NBC Sunday Mystery Movie, which featured *Columbo, McCloud*, or *McMillan and Wife*. Simpler times, you know—great memories.

Sorry, please continue with your story.

While sitting around after a meal one night, one of the elder members of the tribe got—well, let's just call it an idea. "I know; let's let that bear out of his trap. We'll chase him down with our clubs, beat the (bad word) out of him, and have him for dinner tomorrow. How's that sound?"

One of the tribesmen burped, which the elderly human took as an okay to let the bear out. So he did.

Off the tribe went, chasing the poor bear across the stone path, past the creek, up into the woods, and past what would later come to be known as Perimeter Mall. Eventually, though, the bear got to thinking. "What in the (bad word, bad word) world am I doing running? I'm a bear! I can simply turn around, mix these humans with some tree limbs, and make myself a human salad! (Please note that neither ranch nor italian dressings had been invented at that time, so we'll give this bear credit for the invention of the salad. But that's another story).

Why did you leave out Thousand Island on the dressing? That was one of your favorites. And where are you getting this stuff? Please, from your God above, don't blame me for this! I can assure you I didn't put this in your head!

No, this is a true story. If I may, I shall continue.

So it came to pass that at the two-mile point of the run, the bear simply stopped, pivoted, and turned the tables on the really incredibly dumb humans. The clansmen, clubs and all, quickly turned and hauled (bad word) the other way. Circa a mile later (I like to use the word circa, particularly since I'm not really sure what it means), the bear caught his prey, ate some of them, hiked his leg on others, and shooed the rest away.

A bear "hiked his leg"? You've still got Jasper on your mind. Leave Jasper alone—I told you he's got that cured now. Sorry, go ahead.

As it so happened, the first reporter of record happened to be there. We'll call him Fred, especially since that was his name. "Hmm," he said to himself. "They ran two miles out, and then the bear captured the men exactly 1.1 miles later. That's actually five kilometers, if you're going to be quite foreign about it."

Aren't you concerned that you'll tick non-Americans off with this story—especially with your foreign reference?

Since this tale happened at what is now Perimeter Mall in Dunwoody, GA, anything outside of this country would be foreign. Both my readers will totally understand. Besides, political correctness isn't my thing. Well, I take that back. I no longer have my tennis players play king of the court; I call it royalty of the court so as not to offend the girls. Pretty cool, huh?

Please continue with your story. A lacrosse player just scored the winning goal, and I'm going to ignore him for now just to hear the finish of this awful tale. Nothing personal against lacrosse, mind you. Now go on; both readers are dying for the climax.

His wife—Ethel—overheard him. Her reaction was swift. She ran across the yard and beat him over the head with a club. It is to be noted she wanted to be rid of him anyway. He wasn't good at building fires, he was a horrible hunter, and besides, he snored. She then dragged Fred out by his feet and left him by the creek, and Fred now leaves our little tale for the rest of this story.

This Fred is very lucky!

The following week (it might have been a Tuesday, depending on who you ask), Ethel wanted to go for a run to celebrate her getting rid of Fred. "Let's go run a 5K!" she said to her friends. They were confused, because running and distance were rarely put together in the same sentence in those days. Still, Ethel was older; obviously, she had a bit of a temper, and none of the ladies wanted to tick her off. So off they ran.

The group had such a good time that they wanted to make it a tradition. Actually, Ethel had a good time; the rest of the clan was happy simply because Ethel seemed happy. This was a good thing. "Let's get a group together and do this next week," one of them said excitedly. Still, a problem was presented. Since nobody had ever done this before, what would they call it? A dash? A turtle trot? A sprint? A bear blitz? Hmm.

Are you finished?

No, I was just getting started.

Enough! If you want to talk about running or exercise, we can. But please, enough already! The 5K did *not* originate at Perimeter Mall in Dunwoody! You're not even close! Now, what is it you want to discuss about exercise? Or are you just being your normal self and trying to rile me?

Perhaps we should talk about health.

Okay, go ahead. Shoot.

I'm a little injured right now.

What's wrong? What happened?

I find it interesting that God himself has to ask me what happened. Don't you know?

Of course, but I find it way more interesting to get your take on it. Now go ahead; what health issues are you having?

My roommate beat me up last night, and I'm feeling a little sore.

I hate to break it to you, sir, but you don't have a roommate!

I'm talking about your most wonderful invention—the cockroach!

Ah, you had it out with the cockroach again last night. Please tell me about this!

Okay, I'm lying on the couch reading, minding my own business. It was a good book, too, one where the main character was—

Ahem.

Sorry. Anyway, I'm lying about to wrap the book up when the dreaded roach walked out from under my loveseat and casually sauntered right up under me. I mean, I'm on the couch minding my own flipping business and the cocky little guy just ambles over right underneath my face! How gross is that? I mean, I'm getting goose bumps just writing about his!

Understood; now continue.

I immediately went into my best flight-or-fight response. After flexing my muscles, warming up my body, and loosening up my legs, I immediately reached to my end table, picked up a book, and winged it at him!

Did you hit him?

Missed by three feet. The bookmark flew away, the book got damaged, and, what's worse, I have no idea what page I was on!

Jesus wept!

Seriously! Great book, too. It's a young adult book about this teenager who—

Would you please get on with it!

Okay, I'll move on. I think the roach was mad because—I don't know—maybe I forgot to feed him or something. So I got up and ran into my room.

Wow, you are brave!

No, I had to put shoes on. You can never, I mean never, face an angry cockroach without shoes. That actually should be a commandment. Can you imagine how gross it would be to step on a cockroach while barefooted? Imagine what that would actually sound like. I'm creeping myself out just thinking about it!

So you bravely ran into your room and put on some shoes.

Yes, I've got this really old pair of docksides in there. We're talking old. I think I bought them when Jimmy Carter was president; old, old. But I put them on and, clad in only underwear and a pair of docksides, I rushed back into the room.

Disgusting visual, but go ahead.

The roach was just standing there, almost as if beckoning me. He was taunting me. Why, you can get a technical foul for that in the NBA!

For what, walking out from under a loveseat?

No, taunting!

Well, if you forgot to feed me, I'd be pretty mad too.

I approached. This was it: man-to-man, do or die, there is no tomorrow.

Put me down for $500 on the roach, would you?

Wait, I'm not finished.

I'm terribly sorry. Please continue.

I raced across my living room; now I was really mad. To interrupt my wonderful young adult book is one thing. To just stand and mock me in my own house—my own house that I'm only twenty-seven years away from fully paying off—why, that's just downright mean!

What did you do?

I ran across the room, lifted up my left foot in a way that Jasper would've been proud of, and I dropped it down, aiming it directly for his viper-like, tentacle-covered head.

And?

And he simply grabbed my foot, twisted my ankle, and tossed me across the room! Then he pounced on me with his, like, thousand or so legs.

Where can I collect my $500? And will there be a rematch?

Enough! Then he just calmly walked back under his chair as if nothing had happened. Why, if I'd had a date over, that would've been terribly embarrassing.

Yes, *that* would've made it terribly embarrassing.

In closing, I threw my shoe at him, picked up my book, unbent the pages, found my place, and missed the climax of one of my favorite sitcoms. That's simply unacceptable!

Was there a question in this lovely story?

Okay, I guess there is. Why does this getting older thing have to be so tough? I get up in the morning on the day after a run, and I feel like there are rabbits running around in my muscles. Tying my shoe can take a monumental effort, and don't get me started on how I feel once cross-country season starts.

Do you take good care of yourself?

That was my wife's job!

I hate to break it to you, but she tossed you five years ago. Did you not get the memo?

Oh, I thought she was just on a really long vacation. But seriously, is there something we can do to make aging easier?

For one, feed your pet roach! You try going without food a couple of days; you'd be pretty mad too!

Seriously.

After these runs, do you stretch?

Sometimes.

Sometimes! You're asking your body to do the exercise of a twenty-year-old day after day, and you're telling me you stretch sometimes! Okay, then I'll make it so you're not sore ... sometimes.

Cute.

Actually, there are thousands of books out about maintaining good health. Most of you ignore them, some of you read them, and others pretend you'll live forever and simply carry on. I'm not going into detail here. You people take better care—much better care—of your physical possessions than you do your bodies. As for you, have you ever tried yoga?

God recommends yoga?

Yes, God does. We discussed this earlier. Yoga is excellent. It's good for you mentally, spiritually, and physically. Plus, there are usually some hot women in there; the ratio is good enough that even you've got a fighting chance. Well, let's not bring up fighting in your case. Still, stretching, yoga, and maybe even wandering into a weight room every now and then for some circuit training might help.

I used to do that.

And you used to actually have a muscle or two!

Not really. I went up to one of my coaches, flexed my arms to show off, and he immediately informed me that Compound W would get rid of that wart!

I remember; that was cute.

Cute? That killed my spirit.

Don't blame him. You, as always, were looking for a reason to quit going to the weight room.

So I did.

So get back in there! Do yoga. Stretch. Put something in your face besides Tecate, Corona Light, and chips and salsa. Contrary to your belief, chips and salsa are not a major food group! Try fresh fruits and vegetables. Don't make it harder than it is. The older you get, the more maintenance you have to do; not terribly different from the cars you people drive.

I love fruits, but I'm not a big vegetable fan.

Become one!

I used to buy fruit and bring it home all the time! I'd fill up my cart with bananas, grapes, oranges—you name it.

Well, what happened?

The roach kept eating it all.

Mom and Dad

Happy Father's Day!

But I'm not a father.

You want to bet?

This is tough to get used to—being abused by God.

You know I'm kidding, and believe it or not, you are somehow not a father.

I do miss mine, though.

Do you have father issues?

No, not now and not ever. In fact, that's one of my pet peeves; those people who go through their whole lives blaming their parents. Some people literally never get past this!

Look who you're telling!

My dad and mom, though, always rocked. But since it's Father's Day, we can talk about Dad first. He was awesome.

Even when he would throw his smelly socks on your face to wake you up on school mornings?

Man, you saw that? Those were some seriously horribly smelling socks! I'd rather hear my college roommate's alarm clock than smell those things. I'd be awake for the next two days! His socks worked better than all of those Monster energy drinks they sell nowadays at convenient stores.

I actually could smell them from where I'm sitting. Your dad always did have a great sense of humor. Tell us a bit about him. More importantly, tell me your relationship with him.

Okay, let me start with a story about Mom and Dad—and their relationship.

Okay, shoot.

Mom and Dad are in Athens one Saturday night having dinner. Dad is finished eating; he's bored with his company, and he's standing in the parking lot at the car, waiting on Mom. Mom—who never met a person she couldn't strike up a conversation with—is darting here and there, talking, gossiping, laughing. Dad is getting impatient. "Shirley, come on!" he yells. Eventually, Mom does make her way out to the car. She slides into her seat, fastens her seat belt, and she's now officially ready to go. Dad, however, is a bit frustrated. He looks at her and says, "You know, Shirley, one of these days somebody is going to carry you off, do you understand that?" Mom thinks about this for a second, turns to him, and says, "Yeah, but they'd bring me back!"

That's a cute story.

That's a true story! I think that sums up Mom and Dad. The more I hear that tale, the funnier it gets. In fact, not that I want to think about this, but when Mom passes—assuming I'm still around—I'm going to tell that when we're celebrating her life.

You should. Funerals are always much more powerful when their offspring stand up and say a few words. It's a funny statement to make, but it makes for a good funeral. Your dad's funeral, by the way, was good. It was a mix of sadness and humor; he completely appreciated that.

It was a hard thing to do. Usually I look forward to public speaking, though I always get a little nervous. That day, though, was tough times fifty!

But you did it—all three of you boys did it. And the audience loved the part about his smelly socks.

I'm glad they did.

Go ahead, though. Being a God who is sick and tired of hearing people complain about their parents, I ask that you please continue to tell us more about yours. Tell us what it's like growing up in a caring, nurturing family with two adults who completely loved you and did the best they could given what they knew.

You sound like I'm supposed to rub it in for those who didn't come up that way.

No, I merely said it that way because of how I finished the sentence: "given what they knew." Everybody does the best given their circumstances and given what they know and think is right. Come on, as you said, this is Father's Day. Don't rub anything in; just tell me some positives about your home life. I know I've heard my share about the dysfunctional ones. Why, I've got a girl in New Jersey right now lying in the bathtub praying about her mom while her mom is in the living room watching soap operas praying about the girl. They both want each other to change! Good luck with that!
Sorry, I digressed. Tell us a little about your situation.

Well, I've already told you a couple of stories: the Jawja T-shirt Dad had on when he died and the car that cut me off on the expressway after my book signing. Also, I told you the one about the tree branch falling on my head on that non-windy day at the cemetery when I was feeling sorry for myself over the Christmas holidays.

Tell us about the day he went from being your father to being one of your best friends. If I were—gasp—reading this book, I think I'd want to hear that story. If I remember correctly, you actually included that in your speech at his funeral. It was very touching and well received, if I remember correctly.

It was touching for me, but the story itself—unless you were there—comes off very flat.

I beg to differ.

Well, I'm certainly not going to get in an argument with God!

You could if you wanted to, but all I'm asking is that you tell us how your father became your friend. People like to hear these kinds of things. And yes, I will admit some will be a bit envious. But go ahead.

Okay, but the story isn't funny.

What is it with you? Why does everything have to be funny? And why do you think the success or lack of success of what you do is proven by how often people laugh? Though I'm the first to love humor—I even invented it before the 5K came into being at Perimeter Mall—there are serious times. I think a father/son relationship can be one of those.

Well, there were a lot of typical father/son things. He took us fishing, took us to Atlanta Hawks games to watch Pistol Pete Maravich play; he'd throw the baseball back and forth with us in the yard; we went to Braves baseball games. We all went to church as a family.

This was back when you went to church.

I was hoping you were going to let me slide right past that.

Just kidding once again, but let's continue. Once again you are avoiding the issue and the task at hand. Dive in; tell me what I want to hear.

You win. Why did I think I could beat around the bush considering whom I'm talking to. Get the picture: it's 1996 and Dad's wonderful number-three son—that would be me, for those of you scoring at home—is unemployed, dating no one, behind on his rent, flat broke, and borderline depressed. Do not pass Go—though the thought of collecting $200 would have made me jump for joy at the time. Anyway, we had a ritual at home in Madison: whenever I would get up to leave, Mom would walk me to the car, though Dad would just wave from his chair in the living room and let it go at that. In fact, he used to tease Mom: "Shirley, just turn around when you get to the city limits sign, okay?" She would just roll her eyes and then continue walking me to the car.

And?

On this day, however, Dad also got up and walked me outside. This, in layman's terms, was a bit weird. He *never* did that. *Ever!* So there I stood at the car, with my clean clothes thanks to Mom, my $40 in my wallet thanks to Mom and Dad, and my ever-depressing thoughts regarding the pitiful existence that had become my life. I was heading back to—in my mind—a whole lot of nothing: more of the same, ditto, rut, ditto, ditto!

Go on.

Mom was doing her usual stuff, you know, reminding me to brush my teeth and comb my hair, be polite, not scratch myself in public, and look nice. You know, Mom stuff. I was about to open my car door and get in. All of a sudden, Dad walked forward and put his right arm on my shoulder and held it. It was so out of character that it froze me. Hairs shot up on my arms. He looked me dead in the eye and said, "We're with you, you hear?" That was all he did; that was all he said—nothing more, nothing less. See, the story isn't powerful at all.

How about the message?

Oh, my God! Oops, sorry. It was huge! I've got goose bumps again just writing this. That changed *everything*. In the past, my relationship with my dad was similar to when I spoke to a coach or a teacher. You know, I just wanted to tell them what they wanted to hear; that all was right and everything was heading in the right direction—a happy-happy joy-joy kind of thing.

And after that?

After that he became not only my father, but also my friend. I could tell him anything!

And you did, if I recall. However, if you didn't tell him what you just told me before he died, I'm going to come down there and cuff you one.

Yes, I've been told that before, and I'm happy to say I did tell him! I told him a week before he passed. It was the most nervous I've ever been in my life! Ever! And I've been to the free throw line with the game on the line; served at match point, second serve in the third set; pitched with a 3–2 count with the bases loaded; approached a woman at the door to kiss her in hopes she wouldn't turn her head—all that.

We've already discussed your kissing girls on the ear lobes. Enough of that; continue with this story.

Well, he had cancer, and we knew he was going to go any day. Chip, my oldest brother, mailed a letter to him about his thoughts and how much he loved him. You know, the same stuff he said at the funeral. Mark—who shied away from the idea, but that's what made his letter and speech effective, in my opinion—also mailed his in. I, being obviously the most brain dead of the three of us—

Ahem.

Sorry, I will not crack on myself any more. I will not crack on myself any more. I will not—

Get on with it!

Anyway, instead of mailing mine, I waited until I thought he was asleep and placed it next to his bed. There I was, thirty-seven years old and still sneaking around the house. I tiptoed up, placed it next to his coffee mug, and the old fart woke up!

What happened?

He asked, "What is that?" And I know you might find this hard to believe, but I'm one of those guys who simply can't lie. Or if I do, the lie is so dumb or obvious that I might as well just tell the truth. So I told him it was my letter to him.

What did he say?

He said, "Read it to me!" And so I did. It was a two-page letter—the same one I read at his funeral—and it was the longest two pages I've ever read in my life. I was *terrified*! In fact, I think I even had an unplanned bowel movement.

Trust me, God doesn't *even* want to know about that. However, I still don't and can't see why you were terrified; you were doing a perfectly natural and even beautiful thing by telling your feelings toward your father.

But he wasn't that way. I mean, he grew up in New Hampshire. I'm not trying to stereotype, but up there you just didn't say things like "I love you." It just wasn't done. It wasn't natural.

Did you tell him you loved him?

No, I just read the letter—told the part about him touching my arm; told how it changed us. And yes, I did remind him of how bad his feet smelled. I couldn't resist.

What was his reaction?

At first, he didn't react at all. It was probably the longest few seconds of silence in my life—even longer than when I asked my ex-wife if she'd marry me. I placed the letter back on the table and walked out of the room. As I got to the door, however, I heard him say to Mom, "Shirley, read that to me again." I guess I took that as a compliment.

As well you should have. It meant a lot. But continue; we're almost done here, but not quite.

This may be perhaps the strangest thing I've said in this entire manuscript—and I know that's a tall statement—but I feel I've gotten even closer to him after his death.

What if I told you that that's not strange at all—it's common, even. It makes perfect sense. I would only ask that you continue your relationship with him; continue to make it grow. And quit worrying about whether people will think you're weird or not. Guess what, you are weird! Guess what else, so is everyone else down there! I should know! But continue. Let's move on to your mom—I know you have things to tell about her. We can end this chapter with your mom and dad reuniting if you want.

I don't know if I want to go there, because that will mean that Mom's not with us anymore. She's still battling Alzheimer's, and it's a struggle for her—and I know it is for us. As I write this, she might not even know who I am anymore! Do you know how sad that is?

It is, and many people feel your pain. But sometimes when you're not jamming alcohol into your face, you're able to come up with some pretty decent tales. Please continue—we have more to cover here. Hold on, I'll be right back.

Touchdown? Single? Goal?

No, a pregnancy scare.

You answer those, too?

Hey, I'm on call 365/24/7! And to think, some of you people complain even when you're on a vacation! When's mine?

Good Lord!

Thanks! Now go ahead.

I was just going to mention how my mom, too, has always been there when needed. Why, I remember back when I was six—

Oh dear, is this another one of those "A fly ball in Madison, Georgia" stories?

This was deep stuff. If this hadn't happened, maybe I wouldn't have dropped that fly ball!

Yeah, right; keep believing that. Wait! Isn't this chapter supposed to be about family?

I'm family, too, aren't I?

Okay, go ahead. You're six years old. What in the world did you manage to get into when you were six?

Well, the school was putting on this play—a one-act skit entitled *The Vowels*.

Sounds riveting.

Ouch—the sarcasm coming from God! Anyway, my part was to play the letter *A*. I was *so* pumped and excited about it. I had a speaking part and everything. It was a cute little poem, and oh how I practiced and practiced in front of my poor mirror.

I did feel a bit sorry for that mirror, but please continue.

Okay. The plan was for me to nail my part and then woo my friend Connie Shepherd, who was to be sitting in the front row.

So you were planning on riding off into the sunset at the ripe age of six?

Exactly! How did you know? I mean … never mind. Anyway, the day before the play—and I'm talking *the* day before—the teacher gave my part to Terry Armstead. I was crushed; I couldn't be the *A*. She did throw me a bone, however. She gave me the part of *Y*.

What was wrong with that?

Being a *Y* wasn't a speaking part! See? The *Y* was silent! All I got to do was walk across the stage holding my *Y*. No speaking; no words; no wooing; no riding off into the sunset. Heck, the next day Connie gave her dog tag to Bill Ashburn! What kind of world was I to come up in?

I had a twofold agenda there, I must admit.

Please, spill it.

One, I wanted you to get used to getting rejected at an early age. I figured you'd need the practice.

Thanks a lot!

You're welcome. Second, I wanted to cut down the competition in the acting field. With you living in the era of Jack Nicholson, Morgan Freeman, Jim Carrey, and the like, I didn't want them to— you know—have to compete with you for roles. Nothing personal, but I liked Morgan Freeman playing the part of Red in *The Shawshank Redemption*—not you. Again, nothing personal.

None taken.

Okay, let's move ahead. We were moving over to your mom. Didn't you go see her recently? I'm looking for something specific here, so no beating around the bush like you always do.

We did. She's in a home in Butler, Georgia. As my brother Chip says, Butler is a town so small that the city limit sign says "Welcome to Butler" on *both* sides!

Cute, but tell me about your mom.

I hate to be honest, but she was only semi-responsive.

Bless her heart; she's hanging in there. But tell me about the drive home.

Okay, Chip and I were discussing whether she actually knew who we were or not. We sort of went into "poor us" mode. As I mentioned earlier, it is a horrible feeling when your own mother might not know who you are.

Go on; you're getting there. What came out of the conversation?

Well, we did feel sorry for ourselves for a little while, and then we snapped out of it.

How?

I don't remember if it was me or Chip or a combination of the two of us, but the thought was this: Let's say for sake of argument that she *didn't* know who we were. So in her mind, two complete strangers just walked up and sat with her while she was eating her lunch. Instead of getting angry or nervous, she simply looked up, smiled, and sang to us! She sang "Frere Jacques" right then, right there.

And?

And our point was this: She had so many options when the "strangers" sat down. What did she do? She smiled and started singing to us. How *cool* is it to have been raised by *that* lady? How neat is it that? Instead of becoming angry or getting up and leaving the table, she smiled and sang! And we were lucky enough to have been raised by *her*—a lady so peaceful and sweet that the first thing that came into what's left of her mind was a sweet, beautiful smile and a song! And she's our mother!

Did you two cheer up after that?

Of course we did! In fact, I told Chip he'd better tell that story at her funeral. She would love to hear it.

First, he—or one of the three of you—should indeed tell that story at her funeral. Second, the insight you two had about her smiling and singing might be worth the twenty-five cents people might or might not pay for this book. Thanks for including it. I'm not really sure about the rest of the stuff you've included in here, but I'll give you your A you've always been looking for on that one!

Really? So I get my A after all?

You and your brother—I'm not going to send you a certificate or anything. Just know that, in your life, you have made at least one A. Now, let's finish this up—I think my day is about to get really busy.

I won't ask. My only finishing story is how I picture Mom and Dad reuniting when Mom's work here is done. I'm not gunning for another grade on this one—this is simply how I picture things when the two of them meet up again.

Well, get on with it!

Sorry. It's nothing out of the ordinary. I picture Dad standing on the other side of the bridge in heaven—I don't know why I see a bridge, but I always do. Anyway, he wants to show Mom the houses that he's built and the fish that he's caught and stuffed and the paintings he has made and the sculpture of Beethoven he has just finished. It is show-and-tell time, and he simply can't wait to show her, to hold her, to greet her.

And?

And you know Mom. She never met a bridge, a room, or anything that didn't need fixing somehow. So she's taking her sweet time, fixing the flowers, straightening the weeds, cleaning the dust off the "Welcome to Heaven" sign, you name it. I actually laugh as I picture her adding one number to the population sign for heaven. She was a schoolteacher you know; she would do that.

Dad, on the other side, is getting frustrated with her; he's even jumping up and down. I picture him and my dog, Jasper, both waiting for her. It's a cute picture—really cute: Jasper with his tail all wagging, trying to chew off his leash to get to Mom, and Dad getting all worked up. It's a visual I often go to when my mind is going into Crapsville. That and Jasper hiking up his front leg, but we've already discussed that.

And your mom?

Well, she's still being Mom. She's fixing and she's straightening and she's cleaning. At one point, she actually gets down on her knees to fix some flowers. She would do that, too. Eventually, though, she begins her walk; she does so like a golfer who just nailed a drive 280 yards smack down the middle of the fairway. She's fully erect—gallant even—while she strides across that bridge.

Go on.

Well, Dad, as I said, he's lost it a little bit. He grabs her by both shoulders and says, "Shirley, they almost closed the gates. Do you understand that? They almost closed the gates!"

Mom just looks at him with happy tears in her eyes and says, "Yeah, but they'd bring me back!"

Thanks for sharing that story with us. I liked it, and I don't care if it was funny or not!

Happy Father's Day!

Thank you! And thanks for sharing!

Issues with the Commandments

Hey God, I'd like to take issue with you about some of the Ten Commandments.

Oh dear, hold the presses! I knew I forgot to consult you back when those things came out. I actually looked for you; where were you?

Cute—but I think I've obeyed at least some of them. I mean, look at number five: "Honor thy mother and thy father." We just talked about that.

I will admit, you've done better than most at that one. Still, if we took the commandments one by one, this book would be way too long. You might even lose one of your two readers. I myself would get bored, and I invented boredom. And as I mentioned, I've got lots to do! Now I have to listen to politicians praying for votes, for me's sake!

Are politicians—gasp—taking your name in vain? Somehow the Ten Commandments and politicians don't—or shouldn't—go together in the same sentence. Is there a commandment in there about lying?

Even God can't fix politicians, but who are you to rip on the art of lying?

I don't feel like I'm a liar! I remember reading that book *The Four Agreements*, and it said something about being impeccable with your word. It had an effect on me. Plus I'm well versed in not ripping on myself, so I try to make my word count.

Let's get back to lies for a second.

Okay, make your point.

How many Saturday mornings have you woken up, rolled over and said—and I quote—"I will never drink again!"

Oops, I was hoping you didn't hear that!

Do you want the actual count of how many times you've said that? You're forgiven, though. Now let's get back to the commandments. Where are you having a problem? Or shall I say, why should I have included you when the commandments were coined?

Is there any one of us down here who has successfully been sin-free about number ten: "Thou shalt not covet"?

I believe you broke that one the night of your birthday, with your lovely colleague of the last three years.

Am I going to be chunked into hell for that?

What, and waste a perfectly good match! I think the results of that encounter are your punishment in itself, thank you very much.

I can learn to live with that. Still, some of these seem more straightforward than others. I mean, I can perfectly understand number six: "Thou shalt not kill."

That actually should read, "Thou shalt not murder."

So it's okay if I kill my pet cockroach?

That cockroach will once again kick your Georgia butt all across your condo. Are you actually training again for a rematch? Is anyone taking bets? Don't leave me out when the wagers begin!

I'll be ready this time! I'm cross-training.

True, you are. You are jogging, plus you're drinking too much—not a good combination, by the way. There's not a whole lot of life down there that's more confused right now than your very own body.

I stand corrected.

When that roach gets through with you, you won't be standing at all. Now let's get back to the commandments. Is there something you want to ask—or share with me? And please remember, you have to be specific. At last look, your list of Bibles is growing. You've got the King James Version, the New International Version, the New Living Translation, the—

What about number two: "Thou shalt not make unto thee any graven image, or any likeness of any thing that is in heaven above, or that is in the water under the earth"?

You skip around too much! What's wrong with going from one through ten? Are you that whacked? I invented numbers for a reason; you start at the first one and then continue until you reach the last one. Besides, what's wrong with number two?

Well, it goes on to say, and I quote, "for I the Lord thy God am a jealous God."

So?

So I can't picture God being jealous. Why would you be jealous about anything? I mean, you're the same guy that invented hair spray, combination locks, and Monday Night Football. You invented the Rubik's Cube, the NBC Sunday Mystery Movie, and overpriced coffee in airports.

Don't blame me for that! The overpriced coffee was—once again—the invention of you humans. Good coffee should never, I mean never, cost more than two bucks. Keep in mind that I will always factor in inflation. Now that's not going to be the eleventh commandment or anything, but still. Also keep in mind that the simple idea of coffee has gotten *way* complicated these days. Have you been in a Starbucks lately? That's a serious lot of drinks the employees have to memorize! Don't underestimate that, by the way. You could think about reaching into that rickety wallet of yours and tipping them a time or two. They deserve it. And this goes the same for Caribou Coffee and all those other places that serve up lattes, mochas, and the like.

God suggests I tip baristas? And please, you left out Dunkin' Donuts!

Do what you will, but let's get back to jealousy, can we?

You're the boss! I mean, seriously, you really *are* the boss!

What are your questions regarding jealousy? You brought this up earlier in this manuscript.

One, is there a cure for it, and two, do you get jealous?

Let's take number two first—do I get jealous. Let's see, did you get jealous when you saw Bob Thomas kissing Lauren Butterfield in college? Did you get jealous when your brother played with your toy

dump truck while you had to sit in the corner because you had been bad? Were you jealous when—

So you got jealous when you saw Bob kissing her too! She was *way* too good for him! That makes me feel better.

That's not what I meant, and you know it! You should thank me for that, by the way—I spared you a life of divorce and misery.

But I already have a life of divorce and misery!

No you don't—you have a life of opportunity. Besides, where you get your coffee, you're already paying less than two bucks, so quit your complaining! And to top it off, all you have to do is fill out a simple survey and you get your next day's cup free of charge! And you're complaining about it. Did I tell you I hate complaining? *There* is your eleventh commandment: thou shalt quit complaining. *now!*

Okay, we've got Lauren Butterfield and dump trucks and jealousy. Please unravel these mysteries for me. Spare me nothing.

When you get jealous, I am jealous. You humans are a piece of me.

I beg to differ.

You're again going to argue with God? I hate to bring this up, but don't you usually lose when you do that? To use baseball terms, you're batting a grand total of zero!

How am I a piece of you? I mean, haven't you been listening to my tales throughout this manuscript? Haven't you been listening when I've told you of my ADD brain, attempts at relationships and lack thereof? Have I not told you about my being Norm at my watering hole? And how could you possibly forgive me for hiding my Bee Gees and John Denver tapes under my car seat in exchange for the Beatles and Led Zeppelin? When you come down to it, who's to say who's better?

Are you referring to popularity or record sales? I think I'd be a good one to have a say.

True, but you're getting off the subject—if I may be so bold.

You may; you people would do well to be so bold in many cases. I'm not going to restoke the furnace or fill up my gas can when you do that. Questions should be asked. Now, I believe your question concerns jealousy, Lauren, dump trucks, and whether or not there is a cure for the emotion, yes?

Yes, I feel jealousy is a life sentence—incurable. I feel it is a bad thing—*far* worse than the designated hitter, the "quiet please" at tennis matches, and the movie sequel to *Caddyshack*. And that's saying a lot!

Your frustration often thrills me about as much as your ADD-infested skull. I actually applaud anyone who can write about an "incurable" emotion and work *Caddyshack* into the same sentence. In a sick, demented way, you should actually be proud of yourself!

Thanks, I think. But so far you're saying I'm a piece of you—gasp tripled!—and we both get jealous. Will we always be jealous? Is there a cure? Why was that emotion invented? And why did you teach me that lesson with Bob, for heaven's sake? Couldn't you have used a nicer guy? That guy was a tool!

That guy is *not* a tool! For the record, and you usually insist on keeping them, he's doing just as good a job keeping (and breaking) the commandments as you are! Quit judging—there's another potential commandment!

Please continue.

Yes, let me continue while you enjoy your morning coffee. Ahem. When you're jealous, I'm jealous. We are one. I know that literally scares the hell out of you—and I mean that literally—but we are.

You don't want to know where my mind is going right now.

I already know, and you're right, I don't. Please refrain from putting that in here.

Now, is there a cure?

The cure is to take appropriate action, which in your case needs a little work. When you saw your brother playing with your dump truck, you promptly threw your fork at him. This, if I must say, was not appropriate action. When Bob kissed Lauren, you went to the waitress and told her to keep your bar tab open—another dumb decision. How you made it home that night is beyond even me!

Me as well, but don't you see? Jealousy makes us stupid! It makes us do things we'll regret later. So why does it exist? Did you mix the chemicals wrong again? Did God—shall I ask it—make another mistake?

I'm going to stick with cockroaches as my only mistake—and to a lesser degree, ticks. Other than that, my batting average is well over .950, and I'm a bit disturbed you humans haven't put *my* picture on the cover of Wheaties boxes for that. That's a better lifetime average than Lou Gehrig and Babe Ruth put together! I mean, good job of getting golfer Jack Nicklaus on Wheaties boxes, but what about me?

Is God getting jealous?

No, just making a point. And you still haven't discovered the art of taking "appropriate" action. Haven't you heard the saying, "When one door closes, another opens"?

Yes, but those hallways can be awful dark!

Cute and true. But start using jealousy as positive motivation, and also, start using this thing called faith!

So you actually know what you're doing?

I can't believe you just asked me that without fearing that I'd strike you coffeeless and without Tinker Toys for two months and counting! Yes, I *know* what I'm doing—I even knew what I was doing when I invented jealousy.

So jealousy is to be used as a positive emotion? And that doesn't include throwing a fork at my brother?

Truth to be told, your brother was perfectly safe. You never could throw anything straight—you can thank me for that, by the way, though it worked poorly for you in Little League baseball. Did you ever notice how the bleachers were perfectly empty behind the first baseman when you played shortstop?

Great. Part of the master plan, I'm sure.

Sure, but we digress. You needn't be jealous, because you are perfectly capable of accomplishing things in your own right. If it's over something as simple as a woman, haven't you ever heard the saying, "Rejection is protection"?

I must be the most protected soul on earth!

The angels have worked overtime on your behalf; this much is very true. Anyway, the next time you get jealous over something or somebody, I want you to stop and say thank you—just like you do when you hear your very favorite song we've already talked about. Until then, keep hiding your tapes under car seats, freaking out when you hear that song, feeling envious over your colleague, and so forth. One of these years, you're actually going to get it!

You think so?

Let me put it this way: Las Vegas odds give you better odds of that than they do of your chances in your epic rematch!

Is "rejection is protection" another cute way of saying "Thou shalt not commit adultery"? That's number seven, by the way.

Now you are getting it—or at least three of your personalities are. This is great! That also goes under number eight—"Thou shalt not steal"—and that even includes from your buddy Bob!

Okay, enough of the commandments for now. I'm going to leave it alone and actually trust that you know what you're doing!

You're going to trust me, the same being who doesn't read your blog? The same being who had you writing diaries instead of starring on the football field? The same being who had you get pounded at first recess because you watched birds instead of flirting with the cute girls? The same—

I'm going to take that as sarcasm and move on.

Hmm, how can you question jealousy yet leave sarcasm alone?

Good point. Can I ask that we take a break now?

Why?

Because the Braves just got a hit with runners in scoring position. I'll have to take some time to process this.

You're hopeless. But I promise, I love you anyway!

Back at you! And let me take this time to thank you just for being with me all these days.

Trust me, it's been an adventure. Now go forward in non-jealousy and clean your house. Trust me again, no one—and I mean *no one*—is jealous of the condition of your home right now!

I will trust that, and we will talk soon.

I hope so!

God and the Peachtree Road Race

Hey God, will you run the Peachtree Road Race with me next week?

No, I most certainly will not.

Why not?

I don't have a number.

You mean God has to have a number before he can run the Peachtree?

Of course; the Atlanta Track Club has made that very clear. I'm surprised you didn't know this after all these years. After all, the race has been going on since 1970.

That's actually accurate, I think.

It is according to an old article that appeared in the *Northside Neighbor* one summer. It said that the race started in 1970 with 110 runners and that Jeff Galloway, who went on to be an Olympian in 1972, won the race. He ran in Munich with your other hero, Steve Prefontaine.

Hey, I wrote that article!

Oh dear, never mind. It's probably not accurate in that case. Just forget I said anything.

Do I get points for being close? Anyway, come run with me! I'd love to have God at my side while we cruise down Peachtree Street toward downtown Atlanta! Still, I must warn you—there's a lot of drinking and carrying on that goes on along the streets as we run down. Just sayin'.

I might tag along or maybe run it as a bandit, though I don't want to get myself in any more trouble. I've already got a police record going down there. I've still got to do some community service for that substitute teacher thing.

God has to do community service? Didn't you tell them who you were?

Yes, and that made them add more time to my sentence! They thought I was being a smart aleck—and this is after I showed them my ID. After all these years you people have been begging me to make an appearance, what do I get? Jail time and community service! Maybe cleaning up after the Peachtree will be my service; that should take hours upon hours with all the people that show up for that thing!

I don't think the Atlanta Track Club will have you arrested; they'll have more pressing matters on race day. I should've shot you a notice when I signed up in March when the entries came out in the local paper, but of course, I forgot.

That's right, you were away on your little sabbatical, though from what you were escaping I'm not sure. It's okay, though; I might not have heard you anyway. I'm busy in March with every college basketball fan and player sending me signs, shooting their fists at me, and begging me to help them throw that silly orange ball through the hoop. You humans really are amazing.

I'm starting to think you have an issue with basketball.

Not with the game, but what is it with you people and deadlines? I mean, why does March Madness not end until April? What's up with that? And do you realize that right now it's late June and the NBA just got finished earlier this week?

Who won?

Who cares? It's late June! People are vacationing! Something about watching an NBA game while sitting poolside or at the beach just doesn't go together. And it shouldn't! What is it about timetables you people don't understand?

I'm even thinking about sending down this memo I just finished writing:

> **After the taxes are done on April 15, I will *not*—I repeat, will *not*—be taking any more basketball requests. Turn in your uniforms and go play something warm. For any questions or concerns, my basketball office will reopen this October 1, and not a day before. Have a nice day.**
>
> **Love always,**
>
> **God**

I like your writing style, God. You are very straight and to the point. I wish you would've written some of those books I had to read in high school. It seems writers back in the day actually got paid by the word, and man did it ever show!

Leave writers alone! Most of them have suffered quite enough! And look who I'm telling!

Good point, but can we get back to running the Peachtree?

Sure, what do you want to know?

I think it'd be a hoot and a half if you'd run it with me. I'm curious; what kind of pace does God run? What kind of shoes? Are you a Nike man? How about Asics, New Balance, Brooks, Mizuno—which one? Besides, with you at my side, I feel we could win it!

Not a chance! Even God can't run as fast as the Kenyans no matter what kind of shoes I wear. Simply can't be done.

Interesting—even God can't run a sub-thirty-minute 10K. Now I don't feel so bad.

I don't think my 10K personal record is anything anyone should be concerned with. As I've said many times during this manuscript, no one cares about stuff like that except for you. Now what's your issue with the Peachtree?

I'm just not sure I want to run it by myself.

Did you say by yourself? There are going to be, like, sixty thousand people out there; well more than that if you count the bandits and the crowd! What exactly is alone about that?

Wow, even God says "like"; boy, the high school kids are going to love this! You know what I mean, though; I'd like to have someone keeping pace with me, maybe reading me my splits and telling me to speed up or slow down.

I promise you I'll send down all kinds of characters you can run with. There will be one or two dressed like Uncle Sam and many with their faces and bodies painted the sacred red, white, and blue. It will

be sensory overload, as you like to say. I'll even send a group that you can relate to: they will be running as a six-pack. They will even have a little six-pack ring around all of them, so you should feel right at home!

Thanks again, I think.

Once again I say—and once again you won't believe me—I will never leave you alone. And as for my advice: watch out for mile five.

You mean mile four; that's Cardiac Hill.

And that's precisely why I'm telling you to watch out for mile five! You see, everybody knows what Cardiac Hill is—most do, anyway. People get geared up for it, their adrenaline is pumping, and—for the most part—they do a better-than-ample job of getting up it. The problem is, there is a small hill on mile five; that's the one that gets a lot of people.

Why?

Because runners make the mistake of letting their guard down after getting up the big hill on mile four! Don't do that! Stay pumped up; you can relax toward the end. Look at the course as a miniature replica of the Boston Marathon. Perhaps that will help you.

How?

Okay, tell the readers what happened to you the first time you ran Boston.

I was so excited to have finally qualified, to have finally gotten there! I think I peed myself more than twice!

Ahem. Even God doesn't want to know about that, and I consider myself a *very* open-minded God.

Sorry. As for the race, I rocked it—ran a PR even.

Great, now quit bragging and tell them what I'm asking for.

Well, most of the first half—if not all of it—is downhill, and then you start back up. Sort of like the Peachtree, as you said. That part was okay, and then I cruised up Heartbreak Hill! Why, I didn't even know that's what it was until I got to the top of it. I asked the runner next to me if that was it, and he let out a cussing streak a mile long. The gist of what he said was, yes, that was Heartbreak Hill.

Continue; what happened after that?

I relaxed—planned on cruising through the last five miles.

And? You're still avoiding the issue.

Then when I hit the hills on the last few miles, they dang near killed me!

Because you'd relaxed; your guard was down. You weren't mentally prepared. That's why I'm telling you what I'm telling you. You let out your own Tourette's streak as you plodded up the hills on Miles twenty-two through twenty-six. You offended more than one man, woman, and child, I might add.

Sorry about that.

I'm not the one to tell, but it's already forgotten. Just remember that this time—on mile five.

Anything else?

Don't forget your MARTA pass, though you might want to wait a little bit before getting on a train.

Why is that?

Why? Thousands of runners packed like sardines after running on a hot summer's day in July in one car, and you're asking why? Do you remember what your dad's socks smelled like?

That bad, huh?

No, nothing's that bad. Still, you might want to wait a while. Either that or take a taxi back up.

Where should I park my car?

In Atlanta? On a holiday? Parking in that city is bad enough on a regular Monday through Friday. How do you expect me to know where to park on a major holiday with a million people around?

Okay, okay; Brookhaven it is!

While we're at it, watch your diet not just the night before but also the week before!

What's wrong with my diet?

I'm sorry, but the four major food groups are *not* beer, candy bars, pizza, and chips and salsa! This does not work!

It got me through high school and college.

How old were you then? How old did you say you were now? How old would you like to grow to be?

Okay. Diet: check. Parking: check. Marta pass: check. Mile five: check. How about sleeping arrangements? I've often slept at a friend's house closer to the course just so I can sleep in a little more. The problem is, I can never sleep the night before, and I can rarely sleep in a strange bed. What's the big word from God on this?

They say the best night for good sleep is two nights before the race, though I'm still not really sure who "they" are. As for sleeping in a strange house, pack your pillowcase.

Did you say pillowcase? What on earth for?

Because it smells like your sleeping arrangements at home and it's easy to pack! You don't need to bring your whole bed over—this would prove heavy, hard to carry, and perhaps rude. I'm actually laughing as I picture your skinny self toting your entire bed into someone else's home. Pretty funny!

Duh!

Just bring your pillowcase, and put it over the pillow. The smell will remind you of home, hence better sleep.

God, that almost makes good sense!

As you would say, thanks, I think.

It's too bad you won't run it with me. I was looking forward to having your company. Still, I can understand you shying away and everything. I mean, not being able to run a sub-thirty-minute 10K, and also, why would

God want to get beat by a fifty-two-year-old man? Just so you know, I completely understand.

Hold the phone; I'll be right back.

Are you leaving me?

Yes, for the first time ever, I am temporarily leaving you!

Why? Wait. Come back! Where are you going? You just said you'd never leave me and I'd never be alone! Wait!

I'm going to scrounge up a number for the Peachtree!

You mean you're going to let little old me trash talk you into running the Peachtree? You actually let me get to you?

Don't flatter yourself! Still, you're going down, my friend!

Epilogue

It turns out God didn't run the Peachtree. No, it wasn't due to this author's trash talking, or even the heat—it was only seventy-two degrees at the start. It wasn't the crowds he was scared of—seriously, would God be scared of anything? No, in the end his logic was this: "If I get sensory overload as a janitor sweeping up sophomore hall at your school, think what would happen to me if I got in the middle of all that!" I guess he's right—it would be like the time I took my dog Jasper to the Chattahoochee River for a little walk. It turned out to be cute but ... well ... disastrous.

Still, when the afternoon storms were brewing up and I was sitting alone in my kitchen with my glass of wine, I laughed at the mental images of what might have happened—God with a baseball hat on, weaving in and out of the crowds; God accepting water at one of the stops, heading off to a Porta-John and then back onto the street; God with a big smile on his face after crossing the finish line on Tenth Street; God stuck amid hundreds of people on the smelly MARTA train heading back north.

It was at that moment something occurred to me, and I realize anyone who reads this will laugh at the stupidity of it. Still, I'm old enough to realize that when something "feels" right, you either do it or you regret it later. So at that moment I put down my glass of unfinished wine—a miracle in its own right—headed back to my room, and got my Peachtree Road Race sack out of the closet.

True, when many make sacrifices to God, they light candles or put on music, or in Biblical times, they even sacrificed goats. Personally, I've never owned a goat nor quite understood what exactly they did to make us humans so mad. I would light a candle, but being a nonsmoker (thank goodness), I never have any matches. As for music, I've already told you: my iPod got stolen!

In moving on, I opened up my Peachtree sack, threw away my sweaty bib number (kept the pins—I mean, you never know), threw away all the coupons and assorted race paraphernalia, and pulled *the shirt* out. It actually glowed as it sat there on my bed. (Actually it didn't, though often I will take journalistic license for effect. Just go with it.) I lifted *the shirt* sacredly, gently grabbing it on both sides so as not to wrinkle it. Walking slowly and gingerly—okay, that's because I was sore—I put said shirt on my kitchen table. There it lay, nice, clean, and never having been worn.

No, it's not a goat. No, it's not incense. No, it's not music, and I've since forgiven God for not telling me who stole my tunes. No, it is, quite simply, a shirt that I won't describe. After all, if you want a description, then you need to do the race. Telling you what the shirt looked like would be a spoiler; it wouldn't be fair to the sixty thousand plus others who earned theirs.

Anyway, the shirt is for God—my own offering, if you will. I tried to give him my Super Ball as a kid, but I actually forgot to pay for it and got in trouble for stealing. I would've offered my ex-wife, but a man in Washington already has her. I figure he doesn't need a TV; he gets his news even before CNN. In summary, as far as possessions, I don't have much.

But my Peachtree Road Race T-shirt—now *there* is my own personal gift to God. Thank you, God—and I hope you can fit in a large. I thought of this at the finish line, but seriously, what size T-shirt does God wear?

Thanks for listening!

About the Author

Dunn Neugebauer has worked at McDonald's in Athens; tended bar in Rome; checked credit in Dunwoody; written for *NeighborNewspapers* in Sandy Springs; coached tennis in Midtown; substitute taught, coached, and done sports information work in Pennsylvania and at his school in Atlanta; fallen through the roof of his high school in Rutledge; kept stats in Buckhead; been rejected by women in Mexico, California, Nevada, and Canada; worked summer camps in New Hampshire; entered his 150-pound body in a muscle man contest in Florida; gotten lost in London and Edinburgh; run marathons and half-marathons across the East Coast; lip-synched in a choir in Madison; and assembled a two-thousand-piece jigsaw puzzle in Roswell. He currently lives and works in Sandy Springs, Georgia, and is training for an epic rematch with his pet roach. Las Vegas odds say he will lose.

A Final note: If you ever have a question or just want to talk, and God is busy with wars, elections, or athletes who just did something special, you are always welcome to drop several rungs on the ladder and email the author at DNeuge2002@yahoo.com.

- Peace out!